Pictures for the parlour

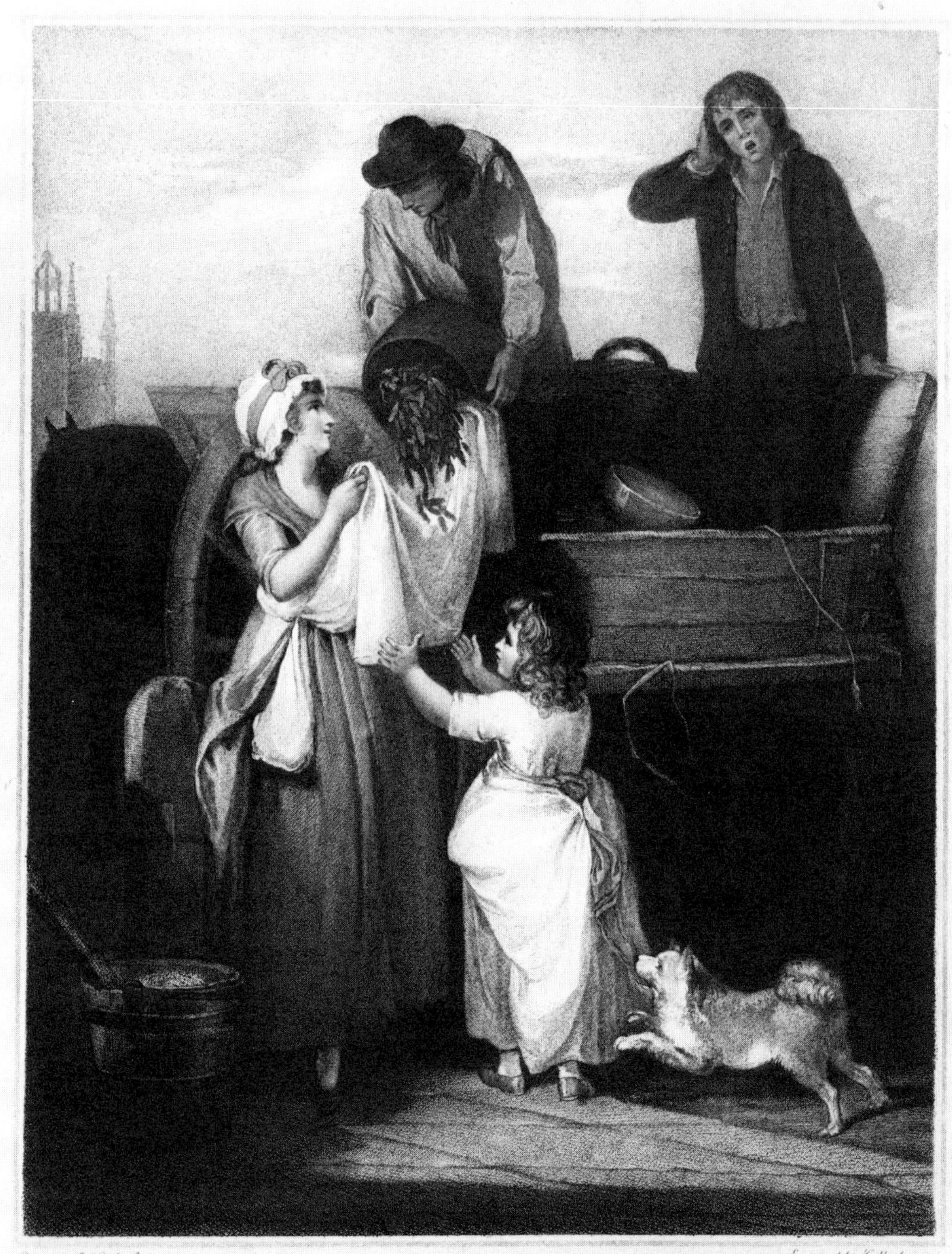

22. Vendramini after Wheatley, *The Pea Seller,* 1795

PICTURES FOR THE PARLOUR

The English Reproductive Print from 1775 to 1900

BRENDA D. RIX

Art Gallery of Ontario
Musée des beaux-arts de l'Ontario
Toronto, Canada

ISBN 0-919876-93-5

Canadian Cataloguing in Publication Data

Art Gallery of Ontario.
Pictures for the parlour

Catalogue of an exhibition held at the Art Gallery of Ontario,
Mar. 12 – May 1, 1983.
Bibliography: p.
Includes index.
ISBN 0-919876-93-5

1. Prints, English – Exhibitions. 2. Art – Reproduction – Exhibitions. 3. Art – Themes, motives – influence – Exhibitions. I. Rix, Brenda. II. Title.

NE628.3.A77 769.941′074′0113541 C82-095258-3

The Art Gallery of Ontario is funded by the Province of Ontario, the Ministry of Citizenship and Culture, the Municipality of Metropolitan Toronto, and the Government of Canada through the National Museums Corporation and the Canada Council.

Art Gallery of Ontario March 12 – May 1, 1983

Graphic Design: Paul Haslip
Typesetting: Techni Process Lettering Limited
Printing: Matthews, Ingham & Lake, Inc.
Binding: Holmes Bindery
Set in Caslon and printed on Dulcet Text and Cover.
All photos by Larry Ostrom, Art Gallery of Ontario.

On the cover:
GEORGE STUBBS (British, 1724 – 1806)
A Horse Frightened by a Lion 1788
Engraving by mixed methods on laid paper
22.8 x 31.8 cm (imp.)
Purchase, 1981

Contents

Preface

PICTURES FOR THE PARLOUR IS ONE IN A CONTINUING SERIES OF EXHIBItions drawn from the Permanent Collection of Prints and Drawings at the Art Gallery of Ontario. It represents a somewhat radical departure from previous exhibitions, however, which have tended to focus on the original print. Reproductive prints, made as copies of paintings or drawings, have received little scholarly attention to date, although many important painters, including Raphael, Titian, and Rubens, recognized the value of such prints in marketing and bringing their art before a wider public. In England, from the late eighteenth to the late nineteenth centuries, engravers working primarily after contemporary paintings, made reproductive prints that catered to the tastes of an ever expanding art audience. In this exhibition, the growing popularity of the reproductive print, its social context and artistic merits are explored within the boundaries imposed by our Permanent Collection.

Brenda Rix, Assistant Curator of Prints and Drawings, has organized the exhibition and written the catalogue. She is greatly indebted to a number of people for their advice and assistance. British scholars David Alexander and Richard Godfrey, authors of the catalogue *Painters and Engraving: The Reproductive Print from Hogarth to Wilkie,* published by the Yale Center for British Art, New Haven, in 1980, laid the groundwork and provided an indispensable source for the late-eighteenth-century section. They made additional suggestions about the content of the exhibition and Mr. Alexander very kindly read the first draft of the catalogue essays. Two other invaluable texts were Mr. Godfrey's *Printmaking in Britain* (1978) and Hilary Beck's *Victorian Engravings* (1973).

We are also grateful to the British Council, who sponsored Mrs. Rix during a two-week stay in England, at which time she was assisted by Reg Williams in the British Museum Print Room and by John Murdoch and Jean Hamilton at the Victoria and Albert Museum. Patrick Noon, Curator of Prints and Drawings at the Yale Center for British Art, New Haven, was very encouraging and assisted with several of the more problematic works in the exhibition. Other staff members at the Center, including Susan Casteras and Joan Friedman, were also very helpful. A number of other scholars who provided information about specific artists were William Pressly, John Riely, Bruce Robertson, and Nicholas Turner.

Mrs. Rix is particularly grateful to Katharine Lochnan, Curator of Prints and Drawings at the Art Gallery of Ontario, who originally suggested the project and has been its enthusiastic supporter, and to Mary-Ann Miller who patiently typed the manuscript. Other staff members have also been involved at various stages; Fred Broun, Barry Simpson, Ches Taylor, Kathy Wladyka, Ralph Ingleton, Susan Douglas-Drinkwater, Maia Sutnik, and other members of the Photographic Services Department and the Reference Library staff. We would also like to thank the editor, Denise Bukowski, and the designer of the catalogue, Paul Haslip.

William J. Withrow
Director,
Art Gallery of Ontario

Foreword

In 1977, with the opening of the second stage of the new Art Gallery of Ontario, the Print and Drawing Collection was assigned greatly increased floor space and equipped with new cabinets and solander boxes. The improved storage facilities enabled us to begin the huge job of reorganizing the thousands of sheets which had come to the Gallery largely by gift from the time of our founding in 1900, and 1975 when the Print and Drawing Division of the Curatorial Department was established.

To assist with this process, a University of Toronto Fine Art graduate student, Brenda Rix, was hired during the summers of 1980 and 1981 under the Experience Program. She took the job in hand, and within a few months had totally organized and integrated the collection by schools, chronologically and by size. Once the mounted, accessioned works had been assigned permanent locations, she was free to begin the task of sorting through the large number of unaccessioned sheets which had been given to the Gallery many years ago, but which at the time of gift had been deemed "study" material.

We began to go through three large groups of prints from the Toronto collections of John Ross Robertson, W.R. Johnston, and F.M. Kimbark. All of these were formed at a time when the word "print" connoted reproductive engraving, and before the late-nineteenth-century cult of the original print had brought reproductive prints into universal discredit. We were delighted to find many important works among the mass of sheets, and began the task of sifting, cataloguing, and accessioning them into the Permanent Collection.

It seems appropriate to draw attention here to the three collectors named above, for they have not been mentioned before in conjunction with the building of the print collection.

John Ross Robertson needs no introduction. A noted Canadian historian and author of the four volume *Landmarks of Toronto,* published in 1917–21, Robertson formed a collection of Canadian pictures which he presented to the Metro Toronto Public Library. He also assembled a collection of about thirty fashionable Victorian engravings, published by the Printsellers' Association in London, which were presented to the Gallery in 1947. This group of proof impressions in mint condition contains a number of works after Sir John Everett Millais by Samuel Cousins, Sir Hubert Herkomer, and other High Victorian engravers.

W.R. Johnston was a clothing manufacturer whose business was ultimately acquired by Tip Top Tailor. Johnston amassed a huge collection of about 800 prints, among them a number of Italian etchings which were included in the 1981 exhibition *The Arts of Italy in Toronto Collections, 1300–1800.* The majority of sheets consist of reproductive engravings from the sixteenth to the eighteenth centuries, among them a number of works by Bartolozzi and his school which are included here.

About F.M. Kimbark we appear to have practically no knowledge, and would greatly welcome information. A member of the Gallery in the 1920s, Mr. Kimbark put together a collection of reproductive engravings and original etchings which ran to hundreds of sheets.

After Mrs. Rix had sorted through these collections, we invited her to organize this exhibition as guest curator while completing her M.A. She has since joined the staff, first as Curatorial Assistant, and now as Assistant Curator, in the Department of Prints and Drawings. She has, in putting together this exhibition, begun the long and painstaking task of interpreting our reproductive print holdings, and of developing her knowledge in an area of neglected, but increasingly important, print history. This is one of the first exhibitions on this theme to take place internationally, and is sure to take its place in the history of the revival of interest in British reproductive prints of the late eighteenth and nineteenth centuries.

KATHARINE A. LOCHNAN,
Curator of Prints and Drawings

Introduction

At a time when originality is perhaps the most sought-after and admired quality in art, the history of the reproductive print has been overlooked by most art historians. The twentieth-century emphasis on the original print has thus cultivated the general belief that engravings made as interpretations of paintings were merely decorative and popular, and has led to the neglect of at least 80 per cent of all prints made in Britain before photography rendered the reproductive print obsolete, and before Whistler and the painter-etchers changed the direction of British printmaking.

The title of this exhibition does little to dispel the suspicion that reproductive prints were collected for their ornamental or decorative value, and for the widespread accessibility of their themes. Prints have traditionally been the most democratic of all the arts, and during the 125-year span covered in the exhibition, images of Old Master and particularly of contemporary paintings and drawings were multiplied and spread farther and in greater numbers than ever before. Their appeal to an expanding art audience represents one of their most vital roles as barometers of taste.

The period from 1775 to 1900 was a time of change and expansion for many endeavours related to the world of art. The growth of public institutions such as the Royal Academy provided opportunities for painters to introduce new subjects and thereby encouraged engravers to develop novel techniques with which to interpret their paintings. Various commercial ventures, the most famous being the Boydell Shakespeare Gallery founded in 1786, were designed to promote both English engraving and painting. John Boydell, in the interests of elevating public taste, commissioned grand paintings of Shakespearean subjects to be displayed in his gallery, interpreted by prominent engravers, and published in several impressive volumes. Seventy years later another great entrepreneur and art dealer, Ernest Gambart, bought painting and engraving rights from artists such as William P. Frith and William Holman Hunt before the paintings were even begun, and he made small fortunes from the sale of engravings alone.

In many instances the dissemination of prints was directly responsible for a painter's fame in his own day, and has saved him from obscurity in the annals of art history. Engravings were responsible for the popularity of such painters as G.B. Cipriani and Francis Wheatley in the eighteenth century, and Sir Edwin Landseer in the nineteenth. The prestige of any painter, even one as great as Sir Joshua Reynolds, was enhanced by the publication of engravings after his paintings.

The intriguing relationship between painters and their engravers has received some recent scholarly attention, but many engravers deserve more recognition. The prints in the exhibition are for the most part works of remarkable technical skill and inventiveness, and some are great works of art. Although engravers usually attempted to copy their models faithfully, occasionally their interpretations were quite free, and presented the public with altered versions of the originals. When close comparison between the model and the engraving or etching has been possible, the various changes have been noted.

The focus of the exhibition is on prints that interpret contemporary paintings, but an attempt has been made to include some works after Old Master paintings and drawings and after contemporary watercolours and drawings. Emphasis has been given to specific areas of reproductive printmaking that illustrate some of its most popular and decorative aspects: stipple engravings of "fancy" subjects and the Boydell Shakespeare Gallery and similar ventures from the eighteenth century, and from the nineteenth century, large Victorian steel engravings that graced almost every parlour.

Whole groups of works that illustrate facets of the development of the reproductive print have been omitted because of lack of availability and limited exhibition space. For example, a greater number of portrait mezzotints and mezzotints of genre subjects would better represent the period. Sporting prints of the late eighteenth century and military and naval prints that were popular until 1815 are also inadequately represented. Caricatures, which were sometimes reproduced by printmakers from designers' drawings, have been considered to be beyond the scope of the exhibition except for two special examples (nos. 11 and 33).

The techniques covered remain for the most part in the intaglio family, with one or two exceptions (see Printmaking Techniques). Examples of reproductive lithography have therefore been omitted, although the importance of the process to nineteenth-century printmaking cannot be denied and some mention of it will be made in the essays. As a topic for detailed discussion lithography was felt to provide enough material for another exhibition.

While not totally comprehensive in scope the exhibition attempts to highlight several of the key artists and important works in the history of the English reproductive print from 1775 to 1900, and to expose to the light of day – and hopefully to the delight of the viewer – many prints that have been hidden away for years merely because they were considered to be "pictures for the parlour."

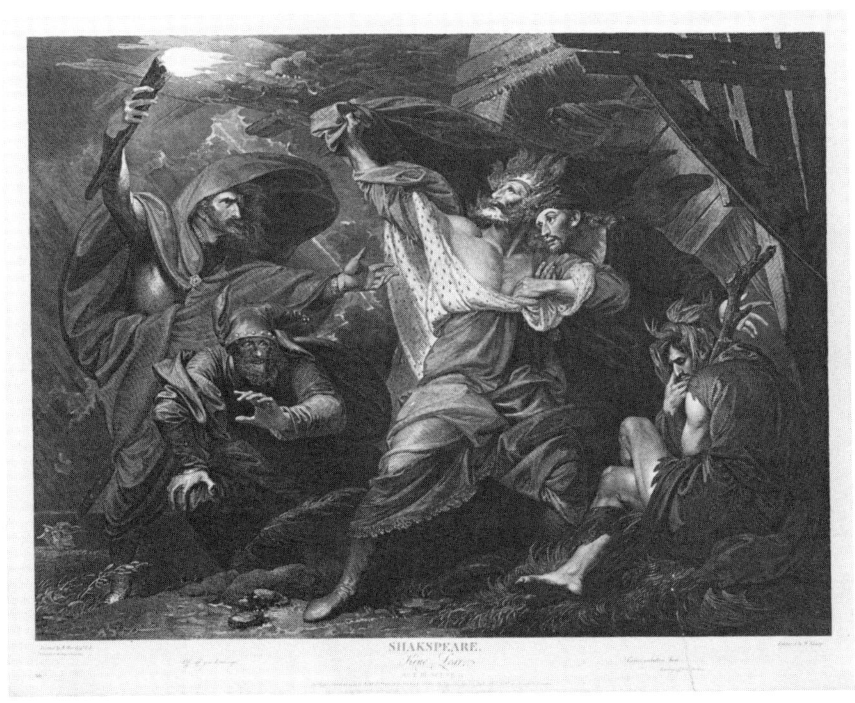

13. Sharp after West, *King Lear, Act III, Scene iv*, 1793

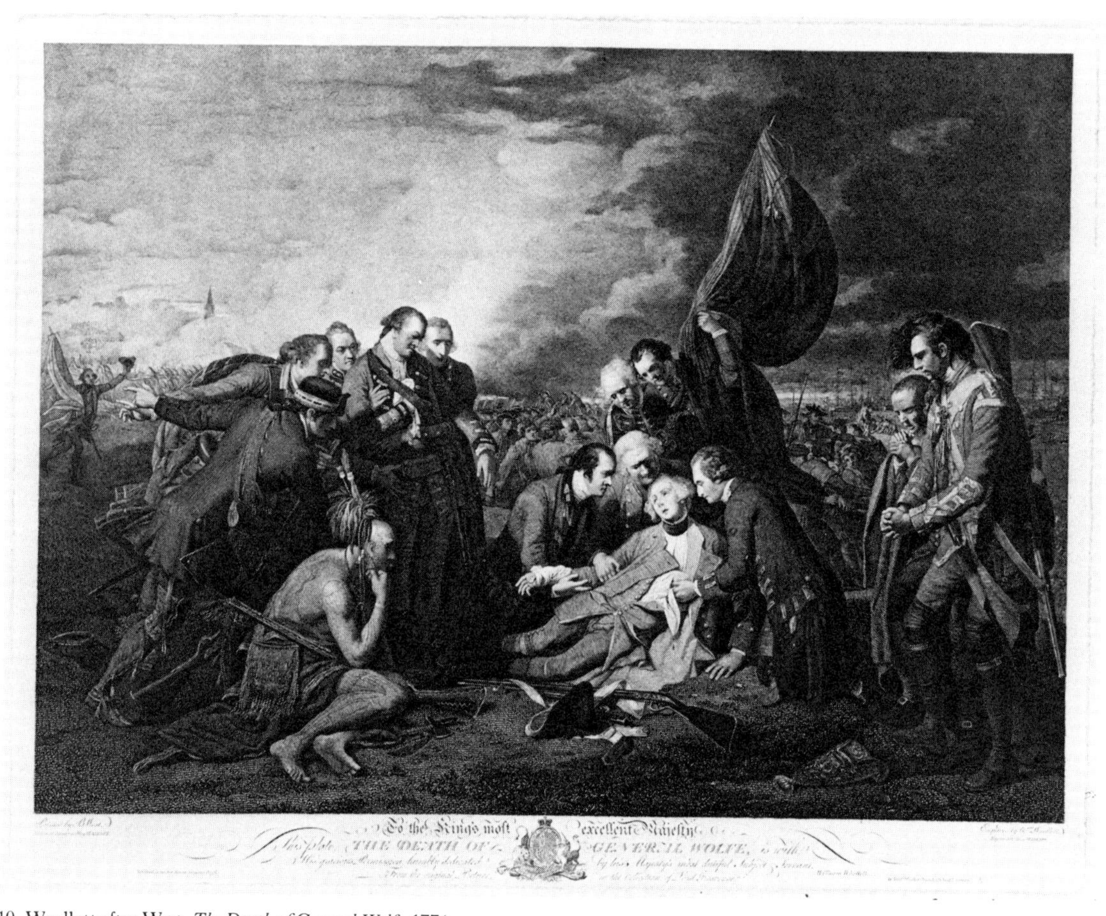

10. Woollett after West, *The Death of General Wolfe*, 1776

The late eighteenth century

An Expanding Print Market

Around the walls are heroes, lovers, kings;
The print that shows them and the verse that sings.
– GEORGE CRABBE, 1807[1]

THE EIGHTEENTH CENTURY WAS THE GREAT AGE OF THE ENGLISH reproductive print. Mezzotint engravings after fashionable portrait paintings largely dominated the market, but new subjects and new techniques began to challenge them seriously during the latter half of the century. Through the establishment of public exhibitions and commercial galleries, and an expanding market for prints at home and on the continent, painters were encouraged to explore genre, sporting, and landscape subjects, as well as themes from history and literature. Translations of their paintings into engravings diffused the fame of painters by spreading their images far and wide.

By the 1760s the traditional processes of line-engraving, etching, and mezzotint were adapted for the new subjects and, by 1775, stipple engraving, aquatint, and colour printing became popular. From light-hearted stipples of rustic subjects to grand patriotic line-engravings of military victories, the variety of subjects and techniques at the end of the eighteenth century makes this one of the most innovative periods in the history of British printmaking.

As early as the 1730s, the artist William Hogarth (1697-1764) was aware of the potential benefit of reproductive prints after his paintings of contemporary subjects. Recognizing the publicity value for his canvases as well as the monetary value of this lucrative sideline, Hogarth personally etched and engraved series such as *The Harlot's Progress* (1732) and *The Rake's Progress* (1735) and supervised the production of the *Marriage à la Mode* series (1745).

In addition, by lobbying for the Engravers' Copyright Act, established in 1735, he made another memorable contribution to the history of prints. The act protected painters against the pirating of engravings and, although in many ways inadequate, it was not substantially amended for over one hundred years.[2] Unfortunately, Hogarth's discovery of a market for prints after "subject" paintings was explored very little by other painters until after the establishment of exhibitions in the 1760s, and particularly after the founding of the Royal Academy in 1768.[3]

Mezzotint

Although English artists throughout the eighteenth century aspired to paint a variety of subjects, portraiture continued to be their most lucrative business. As first President of the Royal Academy, the particular concern of the famous portrait painter Sir Joshua Reynolds (1723-1792) was to elevate public taste through history painting; but he was compelled to compromise by grafting historical setting and detailing onto portraits, because the small elite art audience of the day had little desire to buy grand canvases from English painters, preferring instead paintings by continental artists. Quiet depictions of aristocrats and their families were allotted to artists at home, and the popularity of such portraits in oil and their engraved translations continued unabated throughout the eighteenth century, never completely dying out in the following century. Charles Turner (1774-1857) (No. 4) and S.W. Reynolds (1773-1835) produced mezzotint engravings after Joshua Reynolds in the 1820s and 1830s, while those of Samuel Cousins (1801-1887) were part of a great Reynolds revival in the 1870s.[4]

Called *la manière anglaise* because of its widespread and brilliant handling in England, mezzotint engraving became the preferred process for interpreting the oil portraits of British painters. Soon after its invention in Germany in the seventeenth century, it was heralded by the English as the most perfect of all reproductive techniques, sensitively translating into tone the chiaroscuro effects of oil painting. The softness of the resulting effect was particularly suited to the interpretation of female subjects, as examples in this exhibition reveal (nos. 1 and 2).

Sir Joshua Reynolds, Thomas Gainsborough (1727-1788), and George Romney (1734-1802) were the three most fashionable portraitists in London in the 1770s and 1780s, gaining popularity both through their paintings and the engraved translations. Perhaps because many engraved portraits were published at the expense of the sitter or his family, the eminence of Reynolds' clientele resulted in his becoming the most-engraved painter of the eighteenth century. Approximately four hundred prints were made after his paintings during his lifetime. Gainsborough and Romney had less important patrons, and partly for this reason there are fewer engravings after their paintings. Of the three, Reynolds was also the one most aware of the importance of engravings for his reputation. Gainsborough expressed almost no interest in reproductive prints, although he was intrigued by printmaking techniques and made some original aquatints and etchings.[5]

The earliest interpretations of Reynolds' paintings were made by the Irish engravers James McArdell (c. 1729-1765) and Richard Houston (1721-1775). Their arrival in London in the late 1740s created a revival in the temporarily declining mezzotint market. By the end of the 1750s other Irish engravers appeared, including James Watson (1739-1790) (No. 1), who after McArdell's death became Reynolds' principal engraver for ten years.[6]

After this foundation was laid by the Irish, English engravers such as Valentine Green (1739-1813), Richard Earlom (1743-1822), and William Pether (1731-c. 1816) became very successful in the 1760s, finding new themes, particularly in the subject painting of Joseph Wright of Derby (1734-1797). By 1775 Green, along with Thomas Watson (1750-1781) and John Raphael Smith (1752-1812), took over the portrait market as the Irish influence waned.

Smith typified this new group of mezzotint engravers, executing some splendid prints after both Reynolds and Romney (No. 2). His publishing endeavours, particularly of idealized rustic subjects after the paintings of George Morland (1763-1804), brought him additional recognition. Mezzotints after Morland by the engraver William Ward (1762-1826) and others published by Smith enjoyed great popularity at home and abroad, particularly among those members of the public who wanted "furniture" prints – pictures that could be hung on the wall for decoration. By 1775, to further capitalize on this market, many impressions were hand-painted with watercolour or were expensively printed in colour. In the early nineteenth century, the vogue for prints after Morland and his contemporaries, William Redmore Bigg (1755-1828) and Henry Singleton (1766-1839) (nos. 23 and 24), was eclipsed only by David Wilkie's popular genre subjects.

Stipple

Mezzotint, then, during the last quarter of the eighteenth century, was being used to interpret a variety of new subjects. At the same time, a novel technique was challenging mezzotint in the field of portraiture. Although line-engraving had occasionally been used for English portraits in the past, stipple engraving became the most widely used alternative to mezzotint.

In stipple engraving, tiny dots are multiplied on the copper plate to approximate textures and tonal values. *Mrs. Siddons* (No. 3), by Caroline Watson (1761-1813) after Robert Edge Pine (c. 1730-1788), displays the subtleties that can be achieved by the technique. It is also an example of the theatrical portrait, a subject that had been gaining popularity since the 1760s and the theatrical "conversations" of Johann Zoffany (1734/5-1810). As with mezzotint, stipple came to be used for a variety of subjects, from portraits and furniture prints to Old Master drawings.

Although there were several successful earlier publications of engravings after Old Master drawings, the market for such works flourished towards the end of the century. In France, the fashion for reproductions of drawings of all periods peaked in the 1750s and 1760s. By 1775 British connoisseurs were eagerly buying impressions by English engravers after Old Master drawings, often bound in book form. Techniques designed to reproduce chalk and pen-and-ink were developed first in France and later transferred to England.

William Wynne Ryland (1733-1783) must be given full credit for bringing the crayon-manner and the related stipple-engraving technique from France in the early 1760s. A particularly fine example of the crayon-manner is the *Head of a Youth Wearing a Helmet* (No. 5) from *A Collection of Prints, in Imitation of Modern Drawings,* published by Charles Rogers in 1778. Through tiny dots, Ryland has captured the delicacy and, by printing the work in brown ink, the colour of an original chalk drawing by the seventeenth-century Italian artist, Bartolomeo Schidone. Similarly, the stipple engravings by Francesco Bartolozzi (1725-1815) for John Chamberlaine's *Imitations of Original Drawings by Hans Holbein,* published in 1794, convincingly reproduce the originals.

As illustrated in *Sir Thomas Eliott* (No. 7), printed in three colours, stipple could not only approximate the line and textures of drawing, but in addition was easily colour-printed. Etching was also occasionally adopted to translate drawings, as in Bartolozzi's fine series after Guercino (No. 6). An important distinction should be made between works in this category that often reproduce their models line for line and can be printed in colour on similar paper to the drawings, making them virtual facsimiles; and translations of oil paintings, which are of necessity freer interpretations.

Along with interpretations of Old Master drawings and contemporary oil portraits, stipple engravings proliferated in the area of fancy subjects. Idealized rustic scenes, mythological themes, themes from literature and theatrical subjects, often emphasizing single languorous females or groups of women and children, reflect the taste of the new reading public who were collecting prints primarily for their decorative value (see nos. 18-22). Ryland was one of the first to introduce such subjects into the British print market and is most closely associated with the elegant but rather insipid allegories of Angelica Kauffmann (1741-1807). *Cymon and Iphegenia* (sic) (No. 18), for example, was issued in both black and colour inks. The inscription on the engraving locates the painting in Ryland's collection and designates him as the publisher, suggesting that the original painting was commissioned by him and specially executed to be engraved.

Many stipple prints were made from drawings or paintings designed by a painter specifically for engraving. Previously this had been common practice in the book trade, but was now successfully adapted to the production of wall prints. This category is particularly well illustrated by G.B. Cipriani's (1727-1785) watercolour *The Death of Dido* (No. 19) and the related etching by Bartolozzi (No. 20). Much of Bartolozzi's printmaking effort was devoted to the works of Cipriani. The two artists began a friendship in Italy that was consolidated after their arrival in London in the mid-1760s. Bartolozzi's production, however, expanded far beyond prints after only one artist.

By the 1770s, Bartolozzi had set up a workshop with several assistants and was churning out stipple engravings in the thousands. Composed to a large extent of Italian engravers lured to London by Bartolozzi's success, this studio came to resemble a factory, in which much of the work was executed by assistants with only details and signature added by the master. Many painters, including Kauffmann and Cipriani, worked for printsellers such as Bartolozzi, helping to fill the huge demand for furniture prints among a public who required "undemanding works of art to decorate their rooms."[7] Classic examples of furniture prints were the colour stipple engravings of Francis Wheatley's *Cries of London* (nos. 21 and 22), a series still very popular today.

The ultimate plight of many of these engravings was outlined by Julia Frankau in 1906. By cutting the margins from the prints and framing them close with contemporary mouldings, they could "hold their own with watercolours of the period" and could "be safely hung together with them."[8] Andrew Tuer, from his vantage point in 1885, chronicled the fate of stipple engravings through various changes in taste, from the late-eighteenth-century vogue to the late-nineteenth-century revival:

> Bartolozzi's engravings have literally had their ups and downs: first ascending to the drawing room, later climbing to the bedroom, and eventually to the attic or lumber room, where they remained half or perhaps wholly forgotten, until a revival in taste... brought them down by the same degrees to the drawing room and boudoir.[9]

Of all eighteenth-century reproductive prints, stipple engravings most deserve the appellation, "pictures for the parlour."

Line-engraving

In the hierarchy of eighteenth-century printmaking processes, modelling with dots rated very low in the estimation of many painters and printmakers. It was scorned by the most eminent line-engravers of the day, Sir Robert

Strange (1721-1792), William Sharp (1749-1824), and William Woollett (1735-1785), who maintained the superiority of line-engraving over all other techniques. In the words of Sharp, stipple was characterized by "ease of execution" and was a technique in which "assistants can without any knowledge of drawing, or any Natural taste, perform the greatest part of the labour."[10]

Sharp's condemnation suggests that while stipple engraving, like mezzotint, may have been particularly suited to certain subjects and catered to a wide public, line-engraving, the most laborious and sophisticated of all processes, was deemed most worthy for grand historical themes. The market for line-engraving seems to have been concentrated with the elite, who collected prints in portfolios; but with projects like the Boydell Shakespeare Gallery making history painting more popular, this market was also expanding.

Sir Robert Strange (1721-1792) made valiant but unsuccessful attempts to keep an interest in engravings after Old Master paintings alive (see No. 8). His aim was to "ameliorate national taste" by translating into line primarily sixteenth-century Italian masters.[11] In Horace Walpole's words, Strange "has given us the works of the Italian masters with the tool worthy of Italian engravers."[12] Strange remained inflexible in his belief that the technical skill and control required for line-engraving rendered it the only possible technique for important paintings, although he seems to have modified his regard for the paintings of his contemporaries by executing at least one engraving after Benjamin West.[13]

Recognizing that demand for prints after the Old Masters was negligible, William Sharp occasionally attempted subjects such as the *St. Cecilia* after Domenichino (No. 9), but became best known for engravings after contemporary painters. His *King Lear Act III Scene iv* after Benjamin West for the Boydell Shakespeare Gallery (No. 13) was commended by the painter as one of the best in the entire series.[14] Examination of the *King Lear* reveals Sharp's employment of an elaborate system of parallel lines, dots, lozenges, and cross-hatchings, a system that had been developed and perfected by line-engravers not only to translate the textures and tonal values of paintings, but also to display their virtuoso skill. Employed in the past almost exclusively for the interpretation of Old Master paintings, this sophisticated process, by the 1770s and 1780s was used to tap the new market for patriotic subjects after the paintings of English artists.

Some early manifestations of this shift in taste were William Woollett's engravings after the historical landscapes of Richard Wilson (1713-1782), which gained popularity in the 1760s. Beginning with *The Destruction of the Children of Niobe*, published in 1761, such impressions satisfied the current interest in large prints suitable for framing, gradually replacing engravings after Claude Poussin, Salvator Rosa, and Claude Lorrain. The engraver was called "the immortal Woollett, the Father of English landscape engraving."[15] He encouraged English engraving at a time when many French prints were being imported into England and English line-engravers were extremely under-rated at home.[16]

Woollett's relationship with British painters extended into the realm of history painting, as epitomized by *The Death of General Wolfe* after West published in 1776 (No. 10). This print was "much esteemed abroad"[17] as well as at home and was the "best selling print of the century," with various retouchings of the plate, resulting in several thousand impressions.[18] Based on the success of this publication, engravings documenting military and naval victories became very popular and remained so for the next thirty to forty years.

Printsellers and publishers

William Woollett's success gave courage to his publisher, John Boydell (1719-1804), who was determined to promote both English engraving and English history painting. Boydell had made significant and successful attempts to encourage the exportation of British prints to France since the 1760s, but it is for his Shakespeare Gallery that he obtained the most lasting recognition. Through this gallery he provided a rare opportunity for many contemporary painters who had aspirations to execute history paintings to compete with Europe but who also recognized the financial impracticality when paintings would not sell. Boydell's remedy was to commission paintings after that most dramatic and patriotic of all subjects, Shakespearean drama, which would be exhibited in his gallery, engraved by well known engravers, and eventually published in a multi-volume set of Shakespearean illustrations (see Nos. 12-15). Commercial gain would be made primarily through the sale of the engravings. Boydell published his prospectus in 1786 and opened his gallery in 1789 with thirty-four paintings. By 1791, the first unbound impressions of *The Dramatic Works of Shakespeare* appeared. By 1805, when the gallery was sold, there were 170 works in stock.

Boydell's experiment was rivalled by other similar ventures. Thomas Macklin began his Poet's Gallery in 1788 and Robert Bowyer's Historic Gallery opened in 1793. The current interest in art was reflected by a note in the *Public Advertiser* in 1787 that the "picture mania rages as strongly as the musical mania.... No less than six places are now open for the exhibition of ancient and modern paintings."[19] All three galleries depended upon the sale of engravings for their existence and, as Boydell had hoped, were successful in turning the foreign market around. Another journal of the same year recorded that until "very lately" the supply of prints in Great Britain was obtained from abroad, but the "balance is now turned entirely in our favour" with a significant growth in the export of prints to France.[20]

The eventual failure of all three projects in the early nineteenth century is usually blamed on the advent of the continental wars and the subsequent closure of foreign markets. Serious criticism, however, has been levelled at the prints themselves.[21] Many were executed in stipple apparently because the actual engraving of the plate was faster than line-engraving and much of the work could be carried out by assistants. Unfortunately, the dramatic subjects of the paintings were often unsuited to this technique, resulting in artistically weak prints. Similarly, many of the original paintings were undoubtedly not the most memorable works of particular artists, illustrated by the fact that many are now lost. Despite all criticisms of the works artistically, perhaps the most obvious reason for their eventual unpopularity stemmed directly from the subject matter. The themes of many of the paintings and hence the prints were simply no longer fashionable in the early nineteenth century, when the domestic market was being served by topical military and naval subjects and by topographical landscapes. The ultimate value of ventures such as Boydell's Shakespeare Gallery and his earlier schemes lies in their support and promotion of both painting and printmaking in Britain, encouraging the creation of new art markets at a time when demand had been to a large extent limited to portraiture.

Painters as printmakers

In contrast to the publishing activities of the large printselling firms, three outstanding painters attempted independently to tap the new print market during the last quarter of the century. Paul Sandby (1725-1809), George Stubbs (1724-1806), and James Barry (1741-1806) made prints after their own paintings or drawings by developing very inventive and personal techniques. Their unique approaches to reproductive prints deserve special attention.

Sandby's fame as a landscape watercolourist has sometimes eclipsed his important contribution to the field of printmaking. About 1775, when stipple engraving was the latest fashion, Sandby began "etching in aquatinta," which "if the granulation employed be very minute, will, of consequence, very much resemble a drawing washed with bistre or Indian ink."[22] Invented first in France by J.B. Le Prince, (1734-1781), the tonal capabilities of aquatint were developed further by Sandby, who used it in combination with etching to reproduce the line and the transparent washes of his watercolours, as in *The Entrance of Warwick Castle from the Lower Court* of 1776 (No. 30).

After this initial introduction, aquatint flourished in England for approximately fifty years, sometimes complemented by soft-ground etching, as in Rowlandson's prints after his own drawings and after other artists (No.

31). Other than caricature, landscape was the most popular subject reproduced by the process and books of topographical views with hand-coloured aquatints proliferated in the early nineteenth century.

George Stubbs' early prints were etchings and engravings from his own anatomical drawings for scientific texts. Perhaps his first engraving after one of his own paintings is *A Horse Frightened by a Lion*, published by Stubbs in 1777. Three years later he published a *Leopards at Play*, further illustrating his continued pre-occupation with wild animal subjects.

For several years after these initial publications, Stubbs seems to have been preparing for a concentrated attack on the print market. In 1788 he published at least twelve engravings in his own hand. Also published in that year by Benjamin Beale Evans were two fine mezzotints by his son, George Townley Stubbs (1756-1815) of *Horses Fighting* (No. 25) and *Bulls Fighting* (No. 26). Stubbs' translations of his own paintings, exemplified by *A Horse Frightened by a Lion* (No. 27) and *A Horse Attacked by a Lion* (No. 28), are brilliantly engraved. In his experimental approach to printmaking he rather freely followed the compositions of his paintings, combining several techniques on a single plate with refinement and control to achieve great subtlety of tone and surface. The mood of tension and alarm, balanced by a certain classical restraint and eerie calmness, persists in the engravings as it does in his oil paintings.

Stubbs' engravings are outside any easily defined category, and perhaps because they did not adhere to standard methods for making reproductive prints they were not very widely admired in the eighteenth century, as evidenced by their rarity today. Only in the twentieth century have they come to be appreciated for their originality of expression, and as late as 1908 A.M. Hind omitted Stubbs from his *History of Engraving and Etching*.[23]

Similarly, James Barry's printmaking ventures have received little critical attention until recently.[24] His very bold, almost violent use of the etching needle, accented by scratches from the engraver's burin, contrasts dramatically with the subtle, tonal approach of Stubbs. Barry's earliest prints date to the 1770s and almost all combine etching and aquatint techniques. The translations of his paintings of the *Progress of Human Knowledge* in the Great Rooms of the Society of Arts began to be published in the early 1790s and were his first major prints executed entirely in line.

Lord Baltimore and the Group of Legislators (No. 29) is taken from the *Elysium* and is a particularly noteworthy illustration of his attitude to reproductive prints. Ten years after the completion of the paintings, Barry regretted placing William Penn in a prominent position but was only able to rectify his "mistake" by moving Penn to an obscure location in the etching. Like Sandby and Stubbs, Barry saw his prints as an extension of his work in oil, using them creatively to work out new ideas.

The flurry of artistic activity in London at the end of the eighteenth century was to be somewhat dampened by a brief lull from around 1800 to 1815. During this period painters and printmakers continued to produce, although their energies were channelled into different, and perhaps, quieter, projects. It was left to the Victorians to reclaim the excitement of the eighteenth century, by creating a social and commercial climate in which reproductive prints were in greater demand than ever before.

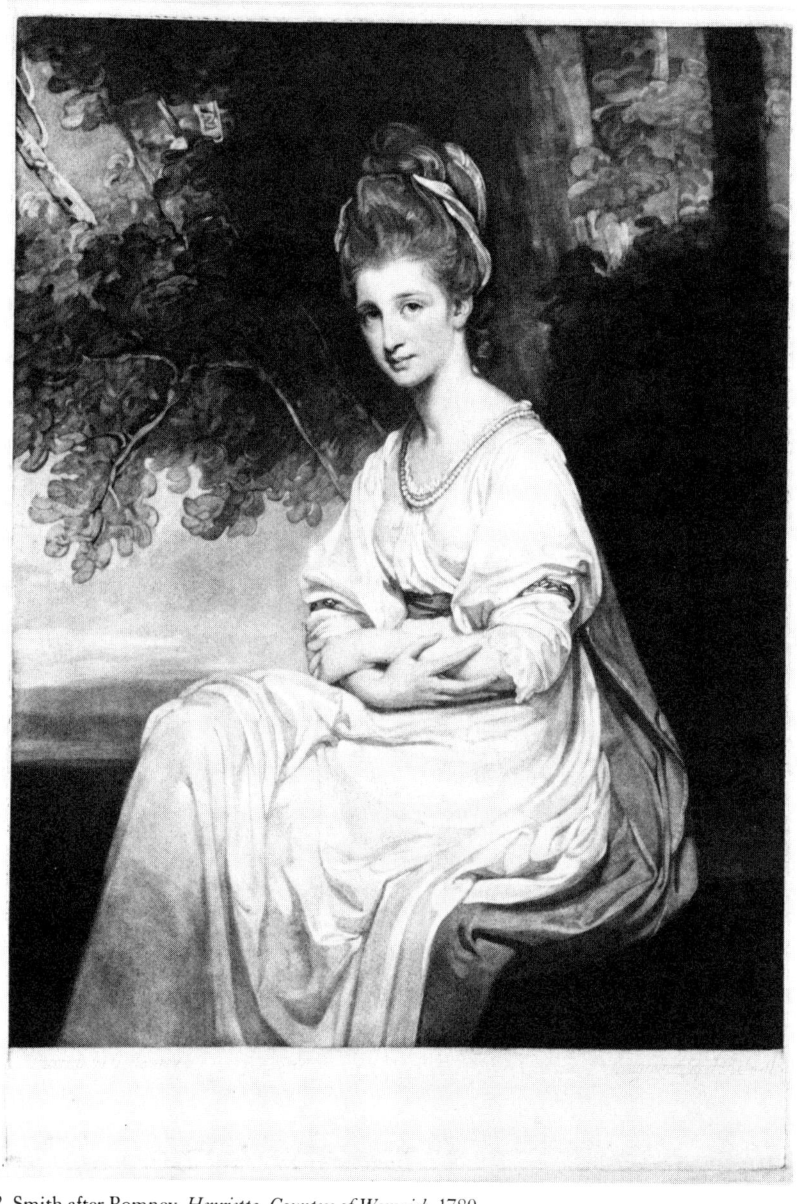

2. Smith after Romney, *Henrietta, Countess of Warwick*, 1780

PORTRAITS IN MEZZOTINT AND STIPPLE

1. JAMES WATSON (British, 1739-1790)
after JOSHUA REYNOLDS (British, 1723-1792)

Margaret Caroline, Countess of Carlisle
1773 C.S. 23 II/2
Mezzotint on laid paper
50.5 x 35.5 cm (imp.)
Purchase, 1982
Acc. no. 82/44

By the 1770s Sir Joshua Reynolds was well established as the leading portrait painter in London. The eminence of his sitters guaranteed that there would be a market for engravings after their portraits among the aristocratic art audience of the day.

Reynolds' painting was probably begun in 1770, the year in which Margaret Caroline, daughter of Granville Leveson, first Marquis of Stafford, married Frederick Howard, the fifth Earl of Carlisle, and it remains in the collection of Hon. Geoffrey Howard, Castle Howard.[25] The compositional format of the painting is characteristic of Reynolds; the sitter is placed beside a large tree in the foreground of the painting, silhouetted against a distant landscape. Her ermine cloak, the rose dangling from one hand and her rather melancholy downward glance, elevate the image above mere "face painting" into a romantic realm.

Chronologically, the mezzotint falls into the earliest period of engravings after Reynolds, which lasted from 1754 to 1775 and which was dominated by Irish mezzotinters living in London.[26] It was engraved and published by James Watson, who arrived in London from Dublin in the late 1750s and was Reynolds' principal engraver from 1765 to 1775. Of the 200 mezzotints that he is known to have completed in his lifetime, sixty-one are after Reynolds' paintings.[27] Ranging in effect from the scraped highlights on the face and dress to the rich blacks of the background, Watson's mezzotint illustrates well the subtle tonal gradations for which the technique was admired.

2. JOHN RAPHAEL SMITH (British, 1752-1812)
after GEORGE ROMNEY (British, 1734-1802)

Henrietta, Countess of Warwick 1780 C.S. 174 I/2
Scratched letter proof
Mezzotint on laid paper
50.2 x 35.0 cm (imp.)
Purchase, 1982
Acc. no. 82/43
ex.-coll. W. Weisbach (Lugt 2659a), Austin Harris

As the third most fashionable portrait painter in London after Reynolds and Gainsborough, Romney did not lack commissions. His subjects were delicate young women and handsome young men who combined "all those neutral qualities which are valued by Society – health, youth, good looks, an air of breeding, or at least of the tone of the highest rank of the social scale,"[28] and their portraits were equally popular in engraved translations, whether or not the sitter was well known.

Henrietta, eldest daughter of Richard Vernon, politician and breeder of famous horses, married the second Earl of Warwick, George Broke, in 1776. Romney has chosen a standard compositional format for her portrait. Seated gracefully in the foreground, she is framed by foliage and a misty landscape in the distance, and seems to represent the essence of aristocratic gentility and ease.

Romney could not have found a more sympathetic engraver for this tender portrait than John Raphael Smith, who was celebrated for his brilliant mezzotint technique. Smith's refined tonal gradations and his choice of soft brown-black ink were particularly suited to the feminine subject.

3. CAROLINE WATSON (British, 1761-1813)
after ROBERT EDGE PINE (British, c.1730-1788)

Mrs. Siddons 1784
Stipple on laid paper
50.8 x 38.0 cm (sheet)
Gift of David Alexander, 1982
Acc. no. 82/78

Theatrical portraits were introduced in the 1760s by Johann Zoffany (1734/5-1810), who illustrated scenes from popular plays featuring, among others, the well known actor David Garrick. Robert Edge Pine also became a leading painter of theatrical portraits; his painting of Mrs. Sarah Siddons (1755-1831) was executed in the early 1780s.

Mrs. Siddons became famous as an actress on the London stage in the 1780s and was one of the most-painted personalities in England during the last quarter of the century. Pine shows her in character as Euphrasia in the tragedy, *The Grecian Daughter*, written in 1772 by Arthur Murphy. She appeared in this play eleven times in 1783; and so this stipple engraving, published by Boydell in 1784, must have been very topical. The scene describes the heroine's murder of King Dionysius in defence of her father, Evander. Pine heightened the drama by the shaft of light that focusses on Euphrasia and by her wild gestures as she proclaims that "in a dear father's cause, A Woman's vengeance tow'rs above her Sex!" Approaching soldiers justify Evander's imploring look toward heaven.

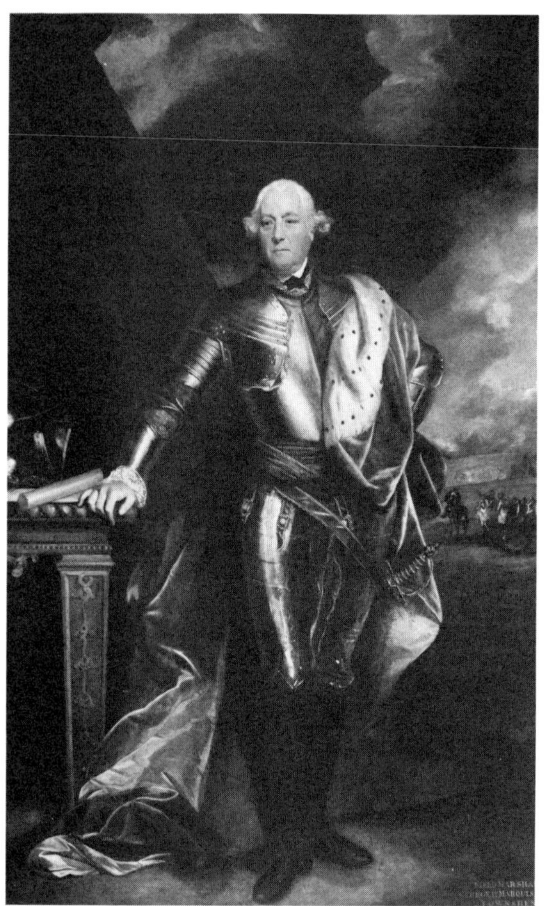

fig. 1. Sir Joshua Reynolds (British, 1723-1792), *Field Marshall George, First Marquis Townshend;* Oil on canvas, 237.5 x 146.1 cm. Purchased by the Reuben Wells Leonard Memorial Fund, Art Gallery of Ontario.

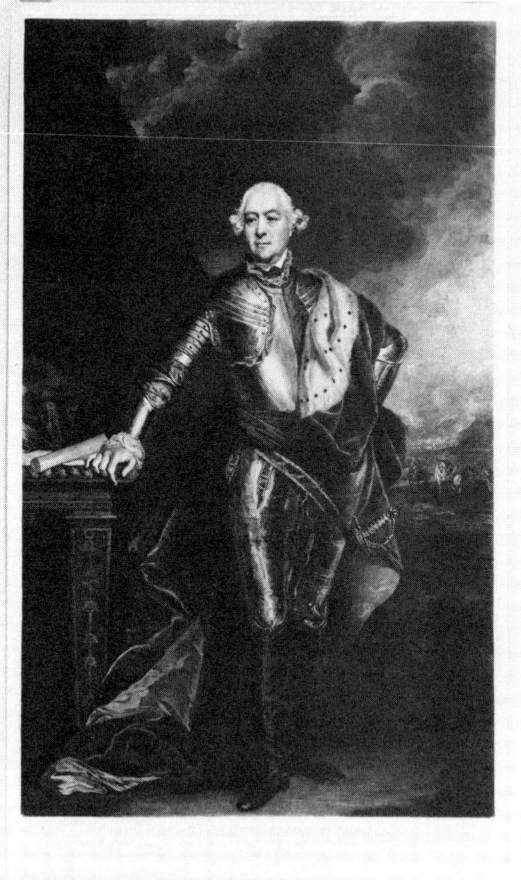

4. Turner after Reynolds, *The Most Noble George Marquis Townshend*, 1807

Caroline Watson, daughter of James Watson (No. 1), received acclaim for her work in both mezzotint and stipple. In 1785, at the age of twenty-five, she was appointed engraver to Queen Caroline. Her stipple engraving of Mrs. Siddons is evidence that by the 1770s and 1780s the technique was being used to interpret a variety of subjects other than standard oil portraits, and that the audience for engravings had expanded beyond a small aristocratic elite.

4. CHARLES TURNER (British, 1774-1857)
after JOSHUA REYNOLDS (British, 1723-1792)

The Most Noble George Marquis Townshend 1807 W. 536
Mezzotint and etching on laid paper
66.0 x 40.0 cm (imp.)
Purchase, 1968
Acc. no. 68/4

The oil portrait of the first Marquis Townshend was painted by Reynolds in 1779 and now hangs in the Art Gallery of Ontario (fig. 1). It is a classic example of the artist's full-length figures, in which he attempts to elevate portraiture to the level of history painting. As in the Lady Carlisle portrait (No. 1), the presence of various props helps to convey the personality and circumstances of the sitter. The Marquis is shown in a noble pose, with one hand placed upon a table embellished with classical motifs. In the background, a battle progressing beneath a stormy sky is a reminder of his military career.

George Townshend (1724-1807) was created a Marquis in 1786, and is a notable figure in Canadian history because he took command of the British troops on the Plains of Abraham after the death of General Wolfe. In addition to his military career, he was also a politician and a talented political caricaturist.

The mezzotint was engraved and published in January 1807, and must have assumed a commemorative value when Townshend died later that year. It admirably approximates all the textures of the original painting, from the gleaming armour to the soft folds of the drapery and the romantic sky beyond. The addition of etching to describe the details of hair, face, and costume places the print firmly in the nineteenth century, when pure mezzotint was to a large extent abandoned by engravers and replaced by a combination of techniques. The etched lines that define the eyes and mouth give the Marquis a slightly leaner, friendlier, and perhaps more youthful appearance than in the painting.

Charles Turner also engraved in stipple and aquatint, and although his reputation is based largely on his mezzotints for J.M.W. Turner's *Liber Studiorium* (No. 34), more than two-thirds of his total output was portraiture.

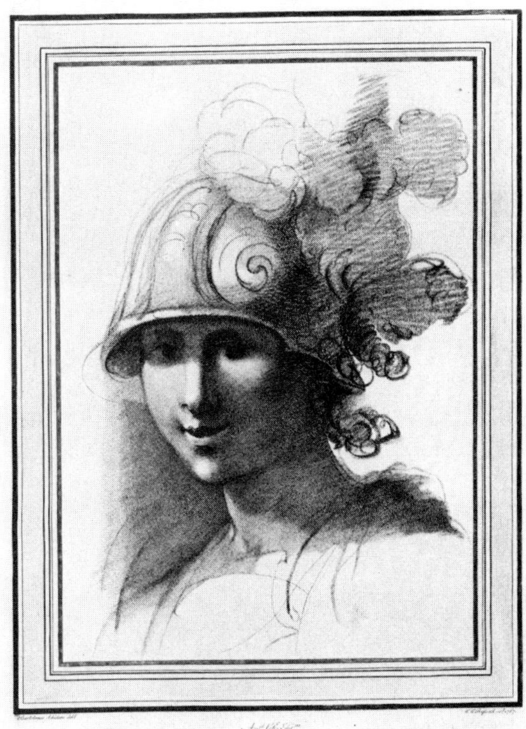

5. Ryland after Schidone, *Head of a Youth Wearing a Helmet*, 1767

TECHNIQUES DEVISED TO REPRODUCE OLD MASTER DRAWINGS

5. WILLIAM WYNNE RYLAND (British, 1733-1783)
after BARTOLOMEO SCHIDONE (Italian, 1578-1615)

Head of a Youth Wearing a Helmet 1767
Crayon-manner in brown ink on laid paper
41.5 x 30.6 cm (imp.)
Presented in memory of W.R. Johnston, 1950
Acc. no. 81/537

William Ryland is almost as well known for his humiliating death by hanging at Tyburn for forgery as he is for his contribution to the field of printmaking: the introduction of the "dotted" techniques into England from France. Ryland learned the crayon-manner in Paris, where it was first used by the engraver J.C. François (1717-1769) in the late 1750s. The *Head of a Youth Wearing a Helmet* was one of his earliest engravings after his return to England in the 1760s, and one of fifty-seven plates by him included in Charles Rogers' *A Collection of Prints, in Imitation of Modern Drawings* published in 1778.

Augmented by etching on the face, the soft dotted lines of the crayon-manner convincingly reproduce the chalk or crayon texture of an original drawing. Probably to further approximate the drawing, the engraving was printed in brown ink. Toward the end of the century, however, engravings in red or brown ink became increasingly fashionable, regardless of the colour of the original.

6. FRANCESCO BARTOLOZZI (Italian, 1725-1815)
after GIOVANNI FRANCESCO BARBERI, called GUERCINO (Italian, 1591-1666)

A Woman Wearing a Turban C. and V. 2165
Etching in brown ink on laid paper
27.3 x 32.0 cm (imp.)
Presented in memory of W.R. Johnston, 1950
Acc. no. 81/536

Bartolozzi learned the fundamentals of engraving and etching in Venice from the engraver Joseph Wagner (1706-1780). In the early 1760s he executed a series of etchings after Guercino which were admired by George III's librarian, Richard Dalton. Dalton subsequently encouraged Bartolozzi to move to London and reproduce the Guercino drawings in the Royal Collection. Arriving in 1764, Bartolozzi apparently began the task immediately. The etchings were subsequently published by Boydell in a volume entitled *Eighty-two Prints Engraved by F. Bartolozzi, from the Original Drawings of Guercino, in the Collection of His Majesty* (1764-1784).

A Woman Wearing a Turban was made after a drawing currently in the Windsor Castle collection (No. 2538), which is drawn in pen and the point of the brush with brown ink.[29] Bartolozzi closely followed the varied width of the lines and free gestural strokes of the drawing. He also adhered to the colour of the original by printing in brown ink.

Reproductive prints after drawings have particular value because the originals were almost entirely inaccessible to all but close friends or acquaintances of the collector. They were usually mounted in albums and were often kept hidden in cabinets. Only through prints, like Bartolozzi's etching, could an interested public have access to such works of art.

7. FRANCESCO BARTOLOZZI (Italian, 1725-1815)
after HANS HOLBEIN (German, 1497-1543)

Sir Thomas Eliott 1794 C. and V. 1124 III/3
Stipple printed in three colours on laid paper
33.5 x 23.5 cm (imp.)
Gift of Mr. and Mrs. Ralph Presgrave, 1978
Acc. no. 78/30

Hans Holbein's chalk portraits of the court of Henry VIII, made as preliminary sketches for oil paintings, were lost for several centuries after their execution. They were rediscovered in 1727 by Queen Caroline in a bureau drawer in Kensington Palace, and are now in the Royal Collection at Windsor Castle.

Soon after their rediscovery two attempts were made to reproduce the drawings through engraving, one by George Vertue and the other by Richard Dalton, the King's librarian; both ventures met with little commercial success.[30] It was left to Dalton's successor, John Chamberlaine, to popularize the images. Chamberlaine commissioned Bartolozzi to interpret the drawings in stipple, printing them in colour to match the originals. They were published in a handsome folio entitled *Imitations of Original Drawings by Hans Holbein* (1792-1800). Since the drawings were not on public exhibition until 1890,[31] the public became familiar with Holbein's work through this publication.

The sitter, Thomas Eliott, was a diplomat, humanist, and author. Bartolozzi's stipple engraving after the Holbein original is a typical example of his somewhat free interpretations of the drawings. Partly because of his late-eighteenth-century perspective, Bartolozzi idealizes the figure, rejecting to some extent the naturalism of Holbein. The definition that he adds to the cloak and the face is also related to the stipple-engraving technique, which lends itself to an increased detailing of forms.

By the 1770s and 1780s stipple was responsible for Bartolozzi's widespread fame. Although the same engraving tools were used in both the crayon-manner and stipple engraving, the latter was designed to approximate the effects of many different media, from chalk to oil paint. It was also eminently suited to colour printing using the "*à la poupée*" method, in which different coloured inks, in this example, black, brown, and rose, were carefully dabbed onto the plate, and the image was printed by a single run through the press. Often etching was combined with stipple. Bartolozzi uses it here to outline the hat and define the long hair of the sitter.

ENGRAVINGS AFTER OLD MASTER PAINTINGS

8. ROBERT STRANGE (British, 1721-1792)
after BARTOLOMÉ ESTEBÁN MURILLO
(Spanish, 1618-1682)

The Young Jesus 1787 Le B.10 III/3
Line-engraving and etching on laid paper
34.5 x 39.5 cm (sheet)
Gift of David Alexander, 1982
Acc. no. 82/77

Robert Strange engraved *The Young Jesus* the same year that he was knighted, making it one of his last engravings. It was intended as a pendant to *Our Saviour Sleeping* after van Dyck and is the reverse of the Murillo painting in the Hunterian Museum and Art Collections, Glasgow. The work is characteristic of Strange's refined line-engraving technique, in which a myriad of fine, closely-laid lines create overall silvery tonalities.

Strange received his early training in Paris, and spent much of his career in Italy and France, where his sophisticated method and choice of subject matter were more adequately appreciated than at home in England. Not deeming either portraits or contemporary history painting worthy of reproduction, Strange dedicated himself to elevating public taste through engravings after the Old Masters. He is also remembered for his attack on the Royal Academy, published in 1775, in which he criticized the institution for excluding engravers from its ranks.[32]

9. WILLIAM SHARP (British, 1749-1824)
after DOMENICO ZAMPIERI, called DOMENICHINO
(Italian, 1581-1641)

St. Cecilia 1790 B.15 V/5
Line-engraving and etching on laid paper
53.5 x 39.6 cm (imp.)
Presented in memory of W.R. Johnston, 1950
Acc. no. 82/82

William Sharp is best remembered for his line-engravings of historical paintings by contemporary artists, but he also interpreted oil portraits and the works of Italian masters such as Guido Reni and Domenichino.

St. Cecilia was described by W.S. Baker as a "noble production" although "stiff and formal in its character and displaying perhaps a little too much of the handicraft of the engraver."[33] Sharp was noted for his sophisticated use of the various line-engraving systems. He was "celebrated for the variety of his stroke-work, which he carefully adjusted to the depiction of different objects."[34] The varying widths of parallel lines and bold combinations of dot and lozenge systems in the engraving of *St. Cecilia* create a richness of texture and a plasticity of form that surpass the work of both Woollett and Strange.

ENGRAVINGS AFTER CONTEMPORARY HISTORY PAINTINGS

10. WILLIAM WOOLLETT (British, 1735-1785)
after BENJAMIN WEST (American, 1738-1820)

The Death of General Wolfe 1776 F.93 IX/10
Line-engraving and etching on laid paper
48.0 x 61.5 cm (imp.)
On loan from a private collection

Benjamin West's painting, *The Death of General Wolfe* was exhibited at the Royal Academy in 1771. It was subsequently purchased by Lord Grosvenor for £400 and now forms part of the Permanent Collection of the National Gallery of Canada, Ottawa. At least three other versions of the painting by West exist: in Kensington Palace, in the Royal Ontario Museum, Toronto, and in the Clements Library, University of Michigan. The many copies by other painters are further evidence of its popularity in the eighteenth century.

The engraving, published by John Boydell, William Woollett, and W.W. Ryland, became the best-selling print of the century, earning large sums of money for its publishers and appearing in thousands of impressions.[35] It also sold well on the continent and copies were engraved in Paris and Vienna.

The painting commemorated the death of the British general James Wolfe on the Plains of Abraham in 1759, a subject that appealed to the patriotic spirit of the day. West's conception was admired for its accuracy in the areas of costume and portraiture, but he ingeniously combined realism with traditional heroic gestures and a lamentation format to create a history painting in the grand manner. When King George III saw the painting he conferred on West the title "Historical Painter to His Majesty." A proof of Woollett's interpretation was similarly admired, and "Historical Engraver to his Majesty" was added to the copper plate for all subsequent impressions.

West's relationship with his engravers was almost unique in the history of eighteenth-century printmaking. He saw them as partners rather than inferior artisans and recognized that he could only be a successful history painter if his works were advertised by the distribution of engraved interpretations.[36] The widespread popularity of *The Death of General Wolfe* helped painters to recognize that the sale of engravings could free them from dependence on portraiture. The success of his partnership with West also convinced Woollett to devote his energies to the translation of history painting, although his landscape engravings had previously received wide acclaim.

The Death of General Wolfe illustrates some of the typical aspects of Woollett's engraving style. In keeping with the practices of most late-eighteenth-century line-engravers he made extensive use of preliminary etching, particularly in his distinctive "worm-lines." He also developed a variety of systems of cross-hatching, of dot and lozenge arrangements, and of long parallel lines alternating with lines of short strokes. Overall, these systems create a strong black-and-white patterning, which is characteristic of line-engraving; but at the same time they convincingly approximate the textures and tonal values of the painting.

11. JAMES GILLRAY (British, 1757-1815)
after BENJAMIN WEST (American, 1738-1820)

The Death of the Great Wolf 1795 BM 8704
Hand-coloured etching on laid paper
29.2 x 43.6 cm (imp.)
Gift of the Trier-Fodor Foundation, 1982
Acc. no. 81/159

The dedication reads, "To Benjn. West Esqr. President of the Royal Academy, this attempt to Emulate the Beauties of his unequal'd Picture, of the 'Death of Genl. Wolfe,' is most respectfully submitted, by the Author." Gillray's etching is, strictly speaking, a reproductive print, albeit an extremely free interpretation of the original. Widespread familiarity with West's painting through Woollett's engraving guaranteed immediate recognition of the source for Gillray's parody. Referring to an attack upon William Pitt in the House of Commons, the etching cleverly satirizes the passing of the Treason and Sedition Bills, while at the same time lampooning the pretensions of history painting.

Gillray began his career as a reproductive engraver but continued to etch caricatures on the side. Eventually, he became one of the first artists to take up political cartooning full-time, a career in which his skill as a draughtsman and etcher was a particular asset. By 1791 all his prints were published by the printseller, Mrs. Humphrey, sometimes in uncoloured impressions but often brightly hand-coloured by assistants. *The Death of the Great Wolf* is a particularly fine impression, hand-coloured using brilliant, fresh pigments.

THE BOYDELL SHAKESPEARE GALLERY AND OTHER PUBLISHING VENTURES

12. RICHARD EARLOM (British, 1743-1822)
after HENRY FUSELI (Swiss, 1741-1825)

King Lear, Act I, Scene i 1792
Stipple on wove paper
50.0 x 62.0 cm (sheet)
Gift of the Library, Art Gallery of Ontario, 1968
Acc. no. 67/57

In 1786 when John Boydell proposed his new scheme to promote English engraving and at the same time encourage a school of history painting, it was welcomed by both engravers and painters. Henry Fuseli became one of his key supporters, completing a total of nine paintings for the project. His *Lear Banishing Cordelia* (fig. 2), now in the collection of the Art Gallery of Ontario, was one of thirty-four paintings exhibited at the opening of the Boydell Shakespeare Gallery in 1789.

Fuseli's devotion to Shakespeare pre-dated his involvement with the Boydell gallery. His unique artistic vision consistently attracted him to scenes of high emotional content and dramatic intensity. Lear's rage as he lunges at Cordelia, banishing her from the kingdom for not matching her sisters' overt protestations of love, was the kind of subject that seemed expressly designed for the painter. According to an account in the *Public Advertiser* in 1789, "it was the privilege of Shakespeare to create; it is the praise of Mr. Fuseli to embody and give form to these creations."[37]

Richard Earlom engraved many oil portraits and Old Master paintings in mezzotint. He is perhaps best remembered for his mezzotint and etching series, after Claude Lorrain's *Liber Veritatis*, published in 1777, although many stipple engravings are also known to be in his hand. His translation of Fuseli's *Lear* displays the qualities of light and shade and the fine detailing possible with the stipple technique. Comparison with the forceful line-engravings in the Boydell series (nos. 13 and 14), however, suggests that contemporary criticism of stippling was somewhat justified. The Earlom print lacks the power and quality of draughtsmanship of William Sharp's line-engraving in particular (No. 13).

A small version of Fuseli's painting measuring approximately the same size as the engraving is now in the Goethe-Museum, Frankfurt. Several details in this small painting and in the engraving are not found in the large canvas. In the center of the image the Earl of Kent's knee is covered with drapery, while in the large painting it is uncovered. Two obvious additions are the crown to the right of the Earl of Kent and a dog in the lower left corner of the image. The close correspondence between the small version and the engraving as well as their similar size suggests that the small painting was the one "copied" by the engraver in his studio. It was not uncommon for painters to provide engravers with reduced versions when their paintings were particularly large and difficult to transport (see also No. 13).

The apparent absence of specific details in the large Fuseli canvas, however, led to a closer examination of the painting and of its history. This research revealed that the work had suffered some deterioration prior to its purchase in 1964 by the Art Gallery of Ontario. Using infra-red light, it was possible to reconstruct some of the missing parts. The dog in the lower left corner and a man's expressive hand above the dog's head, both of which are delineated in the engraving, became clearly visible in the large painting. Some other small details that corresponded to the engraving were also revealed, although neither the crown nor the drapery over the Earl's knee were evident. One can only speculate that they might have been found in the painting in its original condition. This close comparison between the Art Gallery of Ontario's *Lear* and the engraving emphasized the particular value of reproductive prints before the advent of photography. Earlom's engraving recorded, and has now helped to re-construct, the appearance of the original painting.

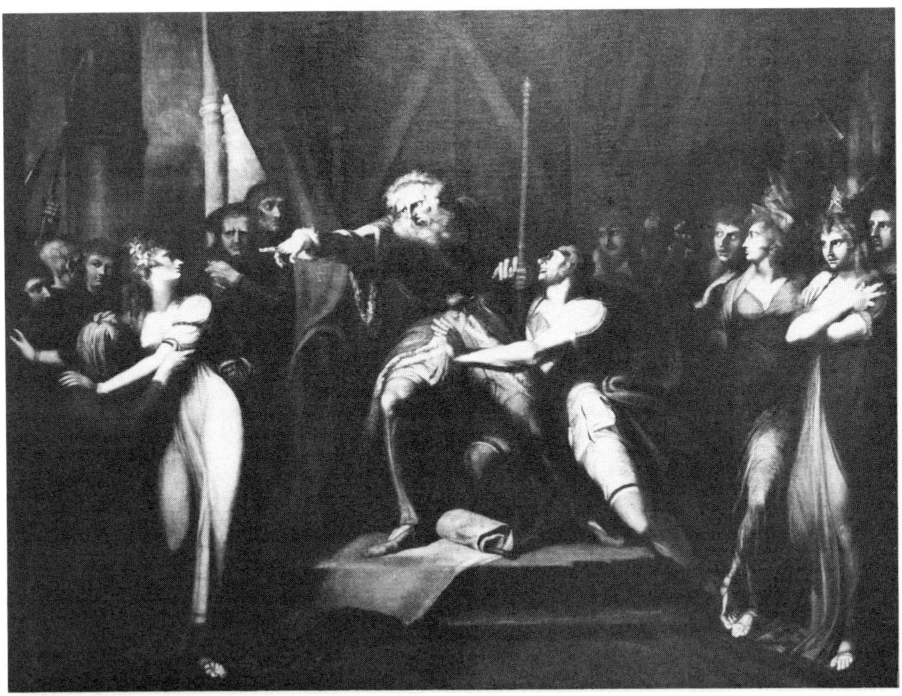

fig. 2. Henry Fuseli (Swiss, 1741-1825), *Lear Banishing Cordelia,* c. 1787-89; Oil on canvas, 267.3 x 364.5 cm. Gift from the Contributing Members' Fund, Art Gallery of Ontario.

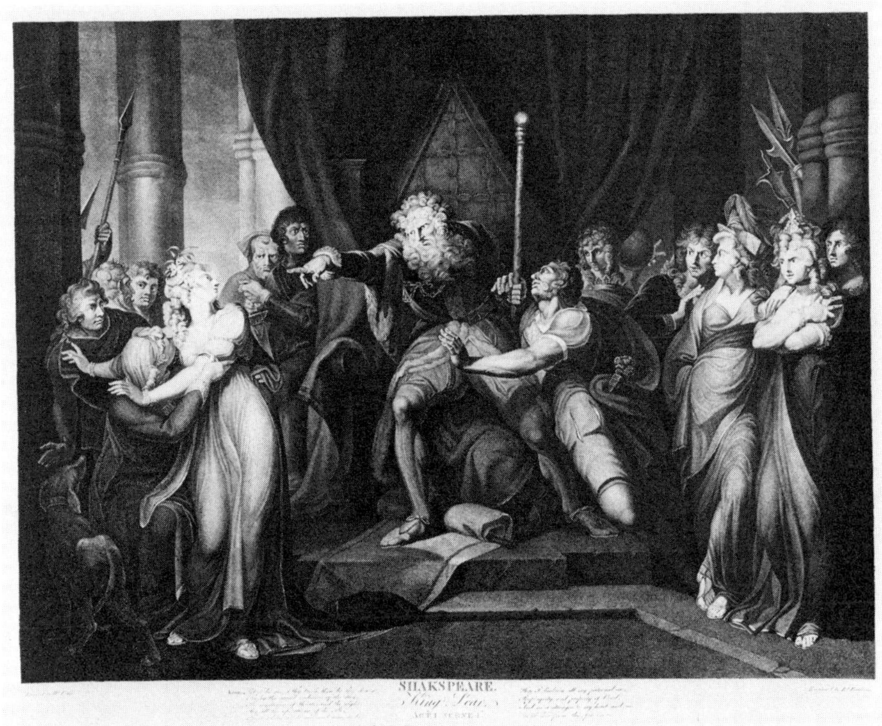

12. Earlom after Fuseli, *King Lear, Act I, Scene i,* 1792

13. WILLIAM SHARP (British, 1749-1824)
after BENJAMIN WEST (American, 1738-1820)

King Lear, Act III Scene iv 1793 B.33 IV/4
Line-engraving and etching on wove paper
49.5 x 63.5 cm (imp.)
Gift of F.M. Kimbark
Acc. no. 81/531

Benjamin West's large painting of *King Lear* is now in the Boston Museum of Fine Arts and a smaller version is in the Museum of Art, Rhode Island School of Design. The latter is approximately the same size as Sharp's engraving and "seems to have been made for the engraver, since all linear details are treated with great care [and it] corresponds exactly to the engraving."[38] Other similar examples (see also No. 12) suggest that when canvases were too large to be easily transported to the engraver's studio, a reduced version was sometimes provided by the painter to aid the engraver in the "copying" process.

West's *King Lear* describes a scene late in the play when Lear, now insane, tears off his clothes, and runs defiantly into the storm. Sharp's interpretation, skillfully drawn and brilliantly engraved, is in keeping with the dramatic power of the painting. In the words of W.S. Baker,

> the 'Lear,' for vigor and originality of execution has never been surpassed, and when West insisted that it should not be engraved in the chalk manner, but in line, and by Sharp, he not only asserted the dignity of his own art, but showed a proper appreciation of the professional excellence of the engraver.[39]

West felt that Sharp's engraving was one of the best of all the Boydell gallery prints, remarking to Joseph Farington that when he had "looked over the Shakespere Prints... [he was] sorry to see them of such inferior quality. - He said excepting that from *His Lear* by Sharpe, - that from Northcote's Children in the Tower, - and some small ones, - there were few that could be approved."[40] The engraving has also subsequently been considered to be the most successful of the Boydell series.[41]

14. THOMAS TROTTER (British, 1750-1803)
after HENRY FUSELI (Swiss, 1741-1825)

Macbeth, Act I, Scene iii 1790
Etching, proof impression on wove paper
48.7 x 63.3 cm (imp. - sheet cut just inside plate mark along top edge)
Purchase, 1980
Acc. no. 80/3

15. JAMES CALDWALL (British, 1739-c.1819)
after HENRY FUSELI (Swiss, 1741-1825)

Macbeth, Act I, Scene iii 1798 First edition

Line-engraving and etching on wove paper
49.8 x 63.3 cm (imp.)
Purchase, 1980
Acc. no. 80/1

As with many other paintings in the Boydell series, Fuseli's *Macbeth* is now lost. The artist chose the "Three Witches" theme several times during his career, attracted by the potential for wild, expressive gesture and dramatic lighting inherent in the subject. The scene describes the horrified surprise of Macbeth and Banquo upon their first encounter with the apparitions.

James Caldwall engraved several plates for the Boydell Shakespeare Gallery. He was assisted in the *Macbeth* line-engraving by Thomas Trotter, who completed the initial etching (No. 14), accurately copying the sophisticated linear systems of line-engraving. Preliminary etching was used extensively during the last quarter of the century to prepare plates for engravers and thereby decrease the length of time required to complete an engraving. In this example it remained only for the line-engraver to fill in the open spaces on the plate with a proliferation of closely placed lines which, particularly in the foreground, obscure much of the detail of the etched state.

Trotter received £210 for his extensive etching of the plate, while Caldwall was paid only £131.[42] A comparison of the two states of the print suggests that the payments were fair remuneration for the amount of work completed by each man. Nevertheless, in keeping with eighteenth-century attitude to techniques, which maintained the superiority of line-engraving over etching, only the engraver's name appears on the published impression.[43]

16. PELTRO WILLIAM TOMKINS (British, 1760-1840)
after HENRY FUSELI (Swiss, 1741-1825)

Prince Arthur's Vision 1788 C. and V. 1430 III/3
Stipple on laid paper
53.0 x 40.3 cm (imp.)
Presented in memory of W.R. Johnston, 1950
Acc. no. 81/513

Thomas Macklin's Poet's Gallery, like Boydell's venture, was an ambitious project designed to promote patriotic subjects by English painters and also to support English engravers. Macklin employed many of the same artists that Boydell had hired for his Shakespearean themes to illustrate "celebrated British poets." Most of the Macklin engravings were executed in stipple.

Inspired by a subject from Spenser's *Faerie Queene*, *Prince Arthur's Vision* is a highly fanciful image. It was one of only two paintings by Fuseli for Macklin and is now in the Öffentliche Kunstsammlung, Basel.[44] P.W. Tomkins, perhaps Bartolozzi's most gifted student, executed many stipple engravings after Angelica Kauffmann and Giovanni Cipriani. Bartolozzi is quoted as saying of him, "He is my son in the art; he can do all I can in this way, and I hope he will do more."[45] Tomkins was one of the few engravers who remained loyal to his master's technique, continuing to use stipple in the nineteenth century.

17. JAMES FITTLER (British, 1758-1835)
after WILLIAM HAMILTON (British, 1751-1801)

Death of Arthur 1793
Line-engraving and etching on wove paper
32.5 x 22.3 cm (image)
Purchased from Alan Garrow, 1969
Acc. no. 81/523

Robert Bowyer issued his prospectus for his Historic Gallery in 1792 with the stated purpose "to rouse the passions, to fire the mind with emulation of heroic deeds, or to inspire it with detestation of criminal actions."[46] To compete with Boydell and Macklin, Bowyer attempted to raise historical subjects taken from David Hume's *History of England* to the level of Biblical and Shakespearean themes.[47] The folio edition, illustrated with engravings after contemporary painters, appeared in nine volumes between 1793 and 1806, and its success reflects an eighteenth-century desire to study the national past.[48]

A particular preoccupation with the Middle Ages was reflected in many of the works and the *Death of Arthur*, with its theatrical lighting and its stage-like setting, is typical of the Bowyer gallery engravings. The murder of Prince Arthur by his jealous uncle, King John, occurred around 1200 AD; David Hume described the event in the following way:

> John first removed him to the Castle of Rouen; and coming in a boat during the night time to that place, commanded Arthur to be brought forth to him. The young prince, aware of his danger, and now more subdued by the continuance of his misfortunes, and by the approach of death, threw himself on his knees before his uncle and begged for mercy: but the barbarous tyrant, making no reply, stabbed him with his own hands; and, fastening a stone to the dead body, threw it into the Seine.[49]

Many of the painters and engravers employed by Boydell and Macklin also received commissions from Bowyer. William Hamilton was one such artist and thus had experience in designing paintings specifically for engraving. James Fittler engraved many other book illustrations, and was very adept in the traditional line-engraving technique.

FANCY SUBJECTS AND GENRE THEMES

18. WILLIAM WYNNE RYLAND (British, 1733-1783)
after ANGELICA KAUFFMANN (Swiss, 1741-1807)

Cymon and Iphegenia (sic) 1782
Stipple on laid paper
36.5 x 31.5 cm (imp.)
Presented in memory of W.R. Johnston, 1950
Acc. no. 81/512

According to the inscription on the stipple engraving, the painting was originally in Ryland's own collection. It is now in the Gibbes Art Gallery, Charleston, South Carolina. The subject was taken from a poem of the same title written by John Dryden in the seventeenth century. Four lines from the poem are also included in the inscription and describe the awakening of youthful love,

> The Fool of Nature, stood with stupid Eyes
> And gaping Mouth, that testify'd Surprize,
> Fixed on her Face, nor cou'd remove his Sight,
> New as he was to Love, and Novice in Delight.

Cymon and Iphegenia (sic) was an amorous and gentle subject, sure to please eighteenth-century audiences. Ryland's fame was based upon such sympathetic translations of Angelica Kauffmann's paintings and watercolours, and she designed many works specifically for his engraving tools to popularize.

Ryland's stipple engraving represents a class of wall-prints or furniture prints that quickly ascended to popularity in the 1770s and 1780s. They often displayed the following characteristics: a pastoral subject printed in monochrome or in several colours, in a round or oval shape suitable for framing;[50] an image that emanated the "sentiment" of the age, soothing the viewer without demanding undue emotional involvement; and a literary, mythological, or genre subject that was easily recognizable by the new reading audience.

Cymon and Iphegenia (sic) is dated to the year that Ryland and Kauffman parted company, and may be the last stipple engraving that Ryland made after one of the artist's paintings.[51]

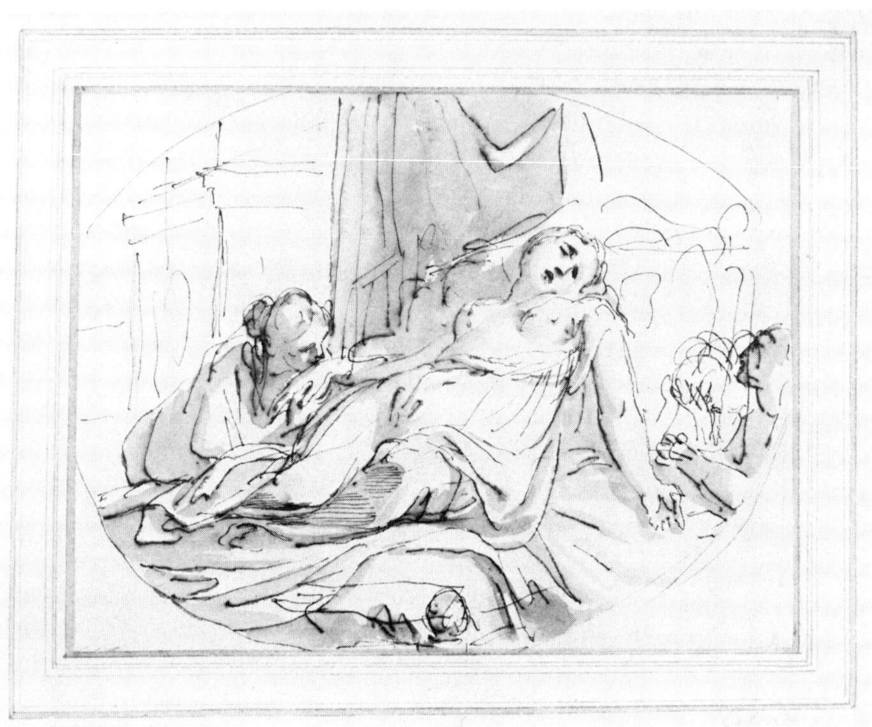

19. Cipriani, *The Death of Dido*

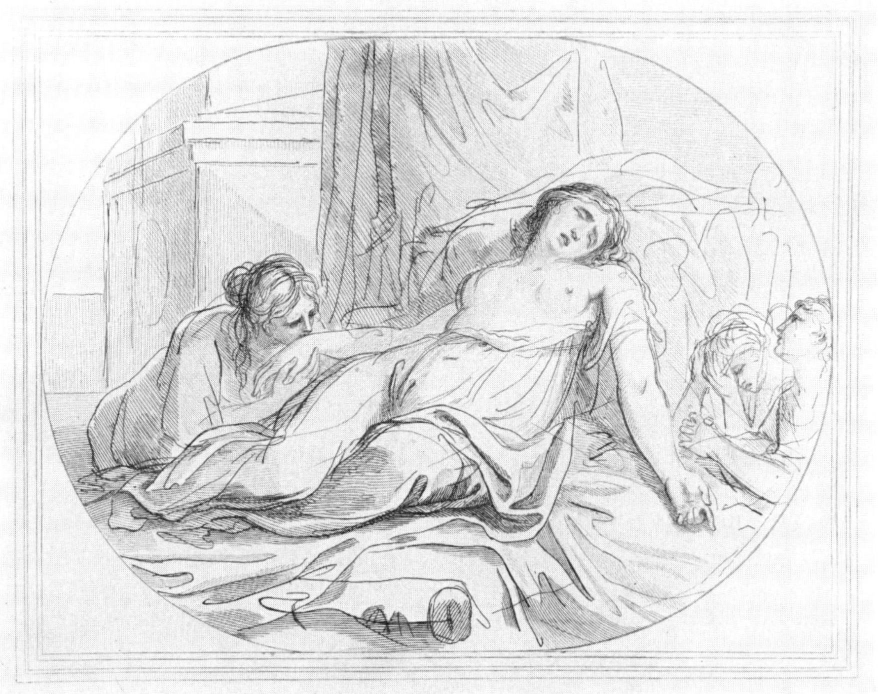

20. Bartolozzi after Cipriani, *The Death of Dido*, 1787

19. GIOVANNI BATTISTA CIPRIANI (Italian, 1727-1785)

The Death of Dido
Pen and brown ink, grey and brown wash on laid paper
22.0 x 26.8 cm
Gift of E.R. Rolph, 1954
Acc. no. 53/33

20. FRANCESCO BARTOLOZZI (Italian, 1725-1815)
after GIOVANNI BATTISTA CIPRIANI (Italian, 1727-1785)

The Death of Dido 1787 C. and V.406 I/2
Etching printed in four colours on wove paper
20.1 x 26.0 cm (sheet)
Gift of E.R. Rolph, 1954
Acc. no. 53/34

Bartolozzi's etching, published by him in 1787, was printed in one colour and, as in this impression, in several colours.[52] A comparison with the watercolour by Cipriani suggests that Bartolozzi has very freely interpreted his model, adding many lines and details not present in the original. The etching belongs to the furniture print category and, if cropped and put into an oval frame, would have provided a delightful wall decoration in an eighteenth-century boudoir.

Most prints after Cipriani were based on wash or watercolour drawings made by him specially to be engraved. His reputation rested primarily on the publication and distribution of stipple engravings by his close friend Bartolozzi. According to Andrew Tuer, "had it not been for Bartolozzi, Cipriani might have attended as chief mourner at the funeral of his own artistic fame."[53]

21. LUIGI SCHIAVONETTI (Italian, 1765-1810)
after FRANCIS WHEATLEY (British, 1747-1801)

The Primrose Seller, Plate 1 from *Cries of London* 1793 W. E.97/III/3
Stipple printed in colour and hand-coloured on wove paper
42.0 x 33.0 cm (imp.)
Gift of Sir Ernest Cooper, 1945
Acc. no. 2813

22. GIOVANNI VENDRAMINI (Italian, 1769-1839)
after FRANCIS WHEATLEY (British, 1747-1801)

The Pea Seller, Plate 7 from *Cries of London* 1795 W.E.107 II/2
Stipple printed in colour and hand-coloured on wove paper
41.5 x 30.5 cm (sheet cut inside plate marks)
Gift of Sir Ernest Cooper, 1945
Acc. no. 2819

Wheatley exhibited fourteen paintings of street-crier subjects at the Royal Academy between 1792 and 1795.[54] Thirteen were engraved in monochrome and in colour between 1793 and 1797 and sold as a set by Colnaghi as *The Itinerant Trades of London in Thirteen Engravings*. The *Cries of London*, as they came to be called, were often re-engraved and copied throughout the nineteenth and twentieth centuries.

Wheatley developed formulas that appealed to wide audiences and much of his work was, like Cipriani's, popularized by the engraver. He specialized in sentimental scenes of rural life or idealized peasants set against the backdrop of the city of London. The attraction of the *Cries of London* stipple engravings lay primarily in their decorative value, but in the eighteenth century the appeal was also partly antiquarian, reflecting a current interest in collecting the old tunes of the street criers.[55]

Schiavonetti and Vendramini were two Italian engravers lured to London by Bartolozzi's success. They became assistants in his workshop and Vendramini took over the business when Bartolozzi moved to Portugal in 1802. Schiavonetti was responsible for the first three *Cries of London* engravings and Vendramini for five of the later ones.

23. ANGELO ZAFFONATO (Italian, d.1835)
after WILLIAM REDMORE BIGG (British, 1755-1828)

The Parent Restored or the Blessings of Peace 1799
Stipple on laid paper
44.5 x 33.8 cm (imp.)
Presented in memory of W.R. Johnston, 1950
Acc. no. 81/515

24. ANTONIO ZECCHIN (Italian, b.1780)
after HENRY SINGLETON (British, 1766-1839)

The Absent Father or the Sorrows of War 1799
Stipple on laid paper
44.5 x 33.8 cm (imp.)
Presented in memory of W.R. Johnston, 1950
Acc. no. 81/516

Although the painter George Morland was largely responsible for adding "rustic genre" to the list of late-eighteenth-century subjects, other artists, including Wheatley, Singleton, and Bigg also capitalized on this market. They chose themes that both idealized rural life and were also patriotic, and engravings after their paintings found a ready market in England and on the continent, as the inscriptions in both English and French attest. To appeal to the increasing demand for engravings among a new reading public, often pairs of prints with contrasting themes or double titles were commissioned by printsellers.

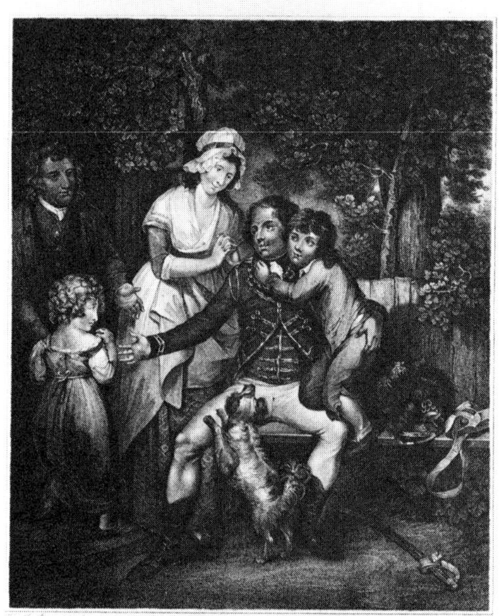

23. Zaffonato after Bigg, *The Parent Restored or the Blessings of Peace,* 1799

Zaffonato and Zecchin are presumably two more Italians drawn to London by Bartolozzi's success. Zaffonato's work is particularly rich, approaching the dark tones of a mezzotint.

ENGRAVINGS AFTER GEORGE STUBBS AND JAMES BARRY

GEORGE TOWNLEY STUBBS (British, 1756-1815)
after GEORGE STUBBS (British, 1724-1806)

25. *Horses Fighting* 1788
Mezzotint on laid paper
48.0 x 59.2 cm (imp.)
Gift of Norcen Energy Resources, Ltd., 1981
Acc. no. 81/2

26. *Bulls Fighting* 1788
Mezzotint on laid paper
48.0 x 59.4 cm (imp.)
Gift of Norcen Energy Resources, Ltd., 1981
Acc. no. 81/1

Horses Fighting and *Bulls Fighting* were painted by Stubbs in 1786, exhibited by the Royal Academy in 1787, and engraved by the painter's son, George Townley Stubbs, in 1788. He worked in both stipple and mezzotint and, among professional engravers, was one of his father's most sympathetic interpreters.

A comparison between the oil painting *Bulls Fighting* (fig.3), which is now in the Yale Center for British Art, and the mezzotint engraving illustrates some general characteristics of reproductive prints. The mezzotint is more detailed than the painting, particularly in the areas of the background foliage and foreground leaves and grass. The colours of the painting have been translated into monochromatic greys and blacks, creating a more ominous, somber mood. Unlike the majority of reproductive prints, however, *Bulls Fighting* and *Horses Fighting* are both mirror images of the paintings. Obviously, Stubbs did not feel that the impact or message of his paintings would be diminished by this reversal (see *Transferring the Image from the Canvas to the Metal Plate).*

GEORGE STUBBS (British, 1724-1806)
after his own painting

27. *A Horse Frightened by a Lion* 1788 T.3
Engraving by mixed methods on laid paper
22.8 x 31.8 cm (imp.)
Purchase, 1981
Acc. no. 81/99

Three versions of the painting are known; in the Yale Center for British Art, in the Walker Art Gallery, Liverpool, and in a private collection. Stubbs first engraved the subject in 1777, placing the horse and lion in a spacious rugged landscape, as in the three paintings. The 1788 engraving omits the landscape and focusses on the psychological drama of the two animals. Stubbs combines realistic detailing, particularly the convincing anatomy of the horse; a romantic sense of terror conveyed by the horse's open mouth and his wildly blowing mane; and a classical sense of balance, created by placing the horse's body parallel to the picture plane like an ancient relief.

His printmaking technique was based on careful craftsmanship and the masterful manipulation of the engraving tools. *A Horse Frightened by a Lion* combines etching, engraving, mezzotint, and stipple to create subtle transitions in tone that approximate the tonal values of painting. Stubbs added drama to the image by silhouetting the frantic white horse against a background of darkness, out of which the placid-faced lion stealthily creeps.

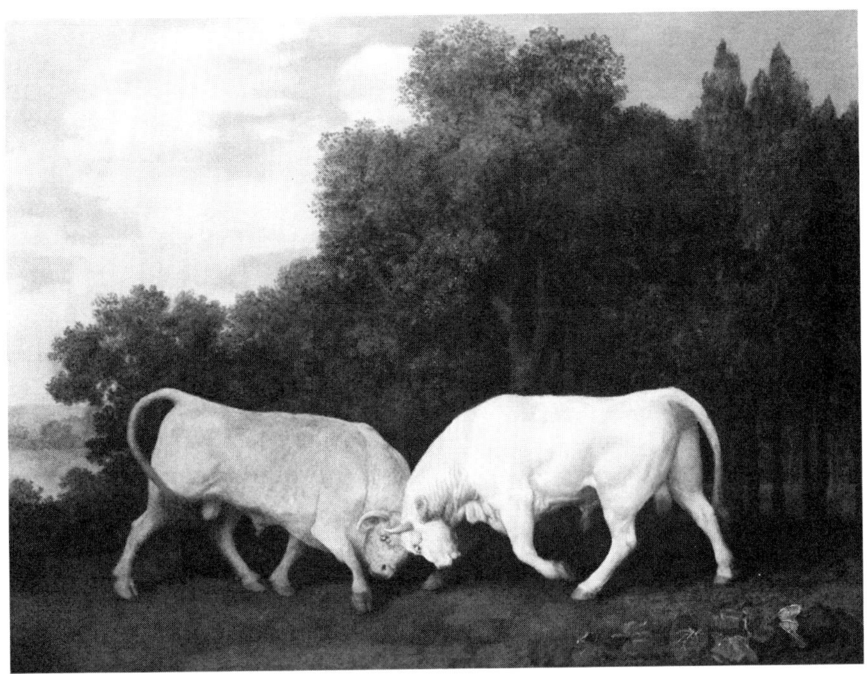

fig. 3. George Stubbs (British, 1724-1806), *Bulls Fighting,* 1786; Oil on panel, 61.5 x 82.5 cm. Yale Center for British Art, Paul Mellon Collection.

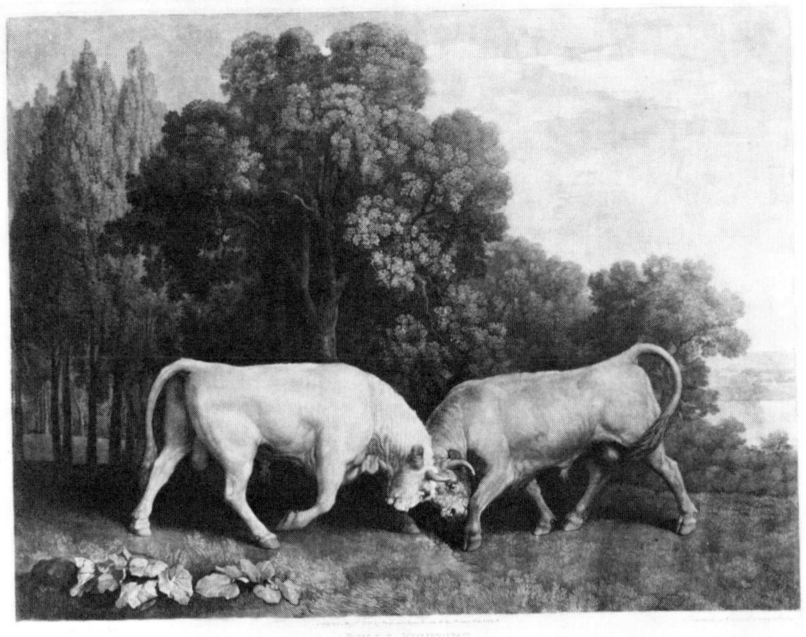

26. G.T. Stubbs after G. Stubbs, *Bulls Fighting,* 1788

28. *A Horse Attacked by a Lion* 1788 T.4
Engraving by mixed methods on laid paper
24.8 x 34.8 cm (sheet)
Purchase, 1982
Acc. no. 82/49

Two paintings of *A Horse Attacked by a Lion* are now in the Yale Center for British Art, one of which is on loan from the Yale University Art Gallery. Another version in the National Gallery of Victoria, Melbourne, Australia, and an enamel-on-copper in the Tate Gallery, London, further demonstrate Stubbs' preoccupation with the horse-and-lion theme. The violence and terror of these animal-combat scenes, combined with a classical timelessness, were key inspirations for French painters, particularly Theodore Géricault and Eugène Delacroix, when they visited England in the 1820s.

As in the previous engraving, Stubbs has reversed the image of the original painting, suggesting that the action could be read from either direction without diminishing the power and impact of the subject. His apparent lack of concern about the reversal may also reflect his experimental and creative attitude to prints, making his engravings to a large extent independent of their models, to be considered as separate works of art.

29. JAMES BARRY (British, 1741-1806)
after his own painting

Lord Baltimore and the Group of Legislators 1793 P.24
II/2
Line-engraving and etching on wove paper
73.5 x 47.0 cm (sheet)
Gift of F.M. Kimbark
Acc. no. 82/80

James Barry was one of the earliest British artists to experiment with aquatint, using it in combination with etching by 1776, the same year that Paul Sandby published his earliest aquatint landscapes (see no. 30). Throughout the 1770s and 1780s Barry reproduced several of his paintings in aquatint and etching and supported himself financially through the private sale of the prints.[56]

From 1777 to 1783 he was occupied with his murals in the Great Room of the Society of Arts, which illustrated the progression of human culture from man's existence in the state of Nature to final retribution. In 1783 he announced a subscription to a series of six prints (later extended by a frontispiece to seven), one after each of the murals. Published in 1792, they were his first major plates executed entirely in line using etching and engraving.

In 1793, Barry began a second series after one of the murals, the *Elysium and Tartarus or the State of Final Retribution*, focussing on various details of the painting. His first plate was *Lord Baltimore and the Group of Legislators*, published in 1793. By 1801 six more details of foreground figures from the *Elysium* were issued. Barry referred to the seven prints as the "large set," as opposed to the earlier "small set" in part because of their relative sizes and in part because he preferred the later works. He said of the later series, "less is lost, and a much more dignified and adequate idea of the work is communicated."[57]

Many of Barry's prints were extensions rather than close reproductions of his work in oil. *Lord Baltimore and the Group of Legislators* was conceived to correct what he by then considered to have been an error in his *Elysium* mural. Lord Baltimore was substituted for William Penn, who had been most prominent in the painting, because by the 1790s Barry considered Baltimore to be the true establisher of a free society in North America.

Barry's later etchings are monumental in conception and bold in execution. His technique is unlike any standard reproductive engraving process and is closer in feeling to the work of the original etcher, John Hamilton Mortimer (1741-1779).

LANDSCAPE AQUATINTS

30. PAUL SANDBY (British, 1725-1809)
after his own drawing

The Entrance of Warwick Castle from the Lower Court
1776
Aquatint and etching on laid paper
33.0 x 46.0 cm (imp.)
Gift of W.B. Dalton, Stamford, Conn., and the United Kingdom, 1964
Acc. no. 64/63

Paul Sandby is credited with establishing watercolour as an independent medium for English painters.[58] His landscape subjects further represent the beginnings of a school of English landscape artists that would flourish in the early nineteenth century, when Englishmen had come to appreciate their own natural surroundings and landscape became a worthy subject for the painter. In addition, Sandby was one of the first artists in England to attempt the printmaking process that most adequately reproduced watercolour and wash drawings.

In September 1775 Sandby wrote to his friend, John Clerk of Eldin, of his progress with the aquatint technique:

> I perceive you have been trying at Le Prince's Secret,...
> I got a key to it and am perfect master of it, you will perceive
> by the inclosed first trials of mine I soon made a progress in

it, I have already done 24 views in Wales and 4 Large Warwicks which I will send you as soon as they are published.[59]

The four views of Warwick were subsequently published by Boydell in 1776 and dedicated to the Hon. Charles Greville, who had provided Sandby with the "secret" of aquatint. Greville is thought to have obtained the secret from the French artist, J.B. Le Prince (1734-1781). In the 1750s Le Prince had devised a method to obtain tonal values by fusing dry powdered resin to the copper plate. Sandby's particular innovation was to mix the resin with "spirits of wine" and brush it onto the plate in liquid form. His subsequent experiments with the lift-ground technique, which he used in combination with etching, helped Sandby to closely approximate the flowing transparent passages and descriptive pen-and-ink lines of his wash drawings.

The publication line on *The Entrance of Warwick Castle from the Lower Court,* "Publish'd Jan.y/1776 by J. Boydell Cheapside," suggests that it is from the first published state. However, Patrick Noon, Curator of Prints and Drawings at the Yale Center for British Art, has compared this impression with one at Yale, and has suggested that it may be from an unrecorded state with touched corrections. An area of the tower appears to have been burnished away on the plate before this impression was pulled, and there are several touches of grey wash on the print that do not appear on the one at Yale. The additions of wash improve the overall composition and quite possibly are in the artist's own hand. Such discoveries illustrate Sandby's experimental attitude to printmaking and his careful manipulation of techniques.

31. Attributed to THOMAS ROWLANDSON (British, 1756-1827) after an unknown drawing

Landscape with Cottage and Trees
Aquatint and soft-ground etching on laid paper
28.0 x 38.0 cm (imp.)
Gift of the Trier-Fodor Foundation, 1982
Acc. no. 81/177

Landscape with Cottage and Trees has not been linked to any specific drawing, although the thick, vigorous line,

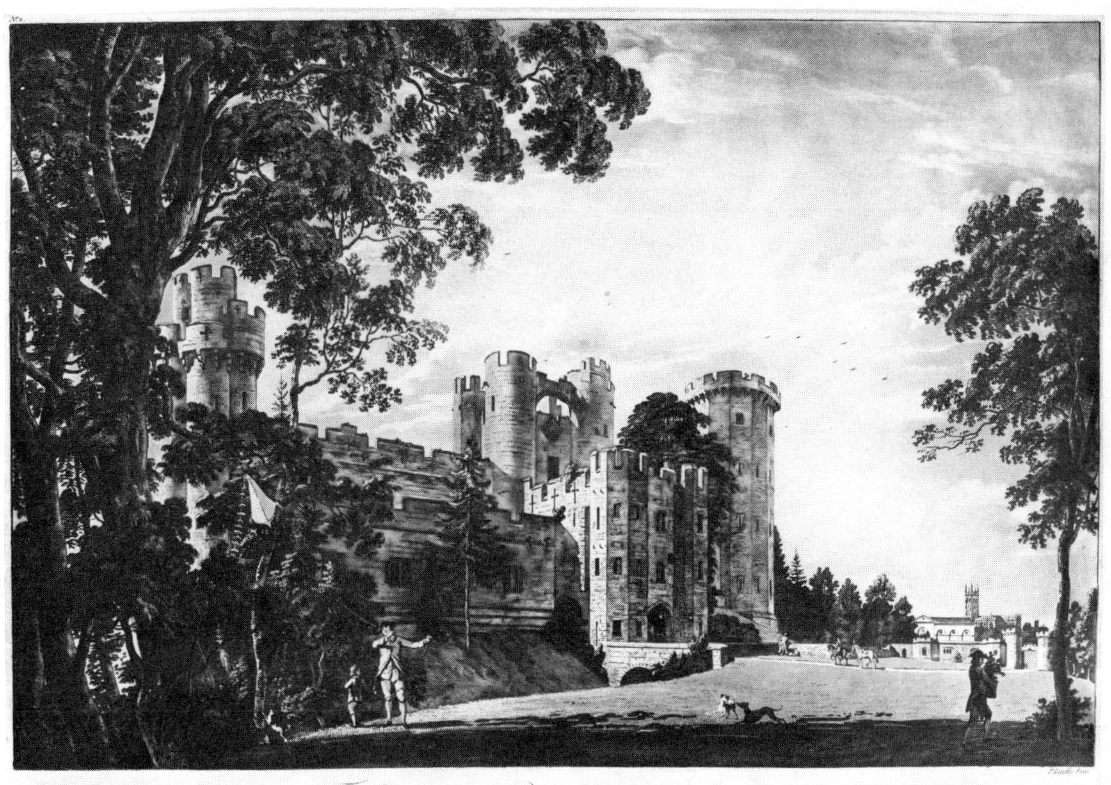

30. Sandby, *The Entrance to Warwick Castle from the Lower Court*, 1776

the dark grey ink used for printing, and the size of the plate are very similar to works after Thomas Gainsborough in Rowlandson's *Imitations of Modern Drawings*, published around 1788. Lacking any inscription or publication line, it appears to be an unpublished print related to the *Imitations* series.[60]

Soft-ground etching with aquatint was particularly appropriate for translations of drawings that used soft graphite or chalk lines with tonal areas of wash.

NOTES

1. George Crabbe, "The Parrish Register," 1807. This poem was drawn to my attention by David Alexander.

2. The act provided protection from piracy of an artist's design for fourteen years. Ronald Paulson, *Hogarth, his Life, Art and Times*, vol. 2 (New Haven: Yale University Press, 1971), pp. 489-90. The act was modified several times in the eighteenth century but it was not until the 1850s and 1860s when agitation from print dealers brought about significant amendments. Jeremy Maas, *Gambart, Prince of the Victorian Art World* (London: Barrie and Jenkins, 1975), p. 110.

3. Exceptions are the Watteauesque fancy subjects in mezzotint after the paintings of Philip Mercier (1689-1760). David Alexander and Richard T. Godfrey, *Painters and Engraving: The Reproductive Print from Hogarth to Wilkie* (New Haven: Yale Center for British Art, 1980), pp. 19-22.

4. Alfred Whitman, *Nineteenth Century Mezzotinters: Samuel Cousins* (London: G. Bell, 1904), pp. 11, 24-25. Whitman notes that S.W. Reynolds was engaged in a task of engraving three hundred and sixty small plates after Reynolds (p. 11). He also discusses the revival of interest in Sir Joshua Reynolds after the Old Masters exhibition at Burlington House in 1870 leading Samuel Cousins to engrave several plates (p. 24-25).

5. Antony Griffiths, "Prints after Reynolds and Gainsborough," *Gainsborough and Reynolds in the British Museum* (London: British Museum Publications, 1978), pp. 32, 39-41. Compared to the more than four hundred prints after Reynolds' paintings engraved in his lifetime, approximately one hundred were engraved after Romney and less after Gainsborough. For information about Gainsborough's original prints see John Hayes, *Gainsborough as Printmaker* (London: A. Zwemmer Ltd., 1971).

6. David Alexander, "The Dublin Group: Irish Mezzotint Engravers in London, 1750-1775," *Quarterly Bulletin of the Irish Georgian Society* XVI (July-September 1973): 84.

7. Mary Webster, *Francis Wheatley* (London: The Paul Mellon Foundation for British Art, 1970), p. 84.

8. Julia Frankau, *Eighteenth Century Colour Prints: an Essay on Certain Stipple Engravers and their work in Colour* (London: Macmillan and Co., Ltd., 1906, first published in 1900), p. 287.

9. Andrew W. Tuer, *Bartolozzi and his Works* (London: Field and Tuer, The Leadenhall Press, 1885), p. i.

10. William Sharp, letter to Mr. Charles Warren, dated 29th May, 1810. Published in H.C. Levis, *A Descriptive Bibliography of the Most Important Books in the English Language Relating to the Art and History of Engraving* (London: Ellis, 1912), p. 97.

11. James Dennistoun, *Memoirs of Sir Robert Strange and his Brother-in-law Andrew Lumsden*, vol. 2 (London: Longman, Brown, Green and Longmans, 1855), p. 259.

12. Ibid., p. 265.

13. This was *The Apotheosis of Prince Alfred and Prince Octavius* after Benjamin West, published in 1786. See Alexander and Godfrey, *Painters and Engraving*, p. 35.

14. Kenneth Garlick and Angus Macintyre, eds. *The Diary of Joseph Farington*, vol. 6 (New Haven and London: Yale University Press, 1979) p. 2331. Entry for May 26, 1804.

15. John Burnet, *Practical Essays on Various Branches of the Fine Arts*, (London: David Bogue, 1848), p. 136.

16. Ibid., p. 137.

17. John Pye, *Patronage of British Art* (London: Longman, Brown, Green and Longmans, 1845) p. 244.

18. Ibid., pp. 249-250. David Alexander, "Painters and Engraving from Reynolds to Wilkie," *The Connoisseur*, CC (January 1979): 61.

19. William T. Whitley, *Artists and Their Friends in England 1700-1799*, vol. 2 (London and Boston: The Medici Society, 1928) p. 71.

20. Ibid., p. 72

21. See Winifred Friedman, "Some Commercial Aspects of the Boydell Shakespeare Gallery" *Journal of the Warburg and Courtauld Institutes* XXXVI (1973): 396-401 for a description of the controversy surrounding the closure of the Boydell Gallery.

22. John Landseer, *Lectures on the Art of Engraving* (London: Longman, Hurst, Rees and Orme, 1807), p. 132.

23. Basil Taylor, *The Prints of George Stubbs* (London: Phaidon Press, 1971), p. 5. See also Richard T. Godfrey, "George Stubbs as a Printmaker," *The Print Collector's Newsletter* XIII (September-October 1982): 113-116.

24. See William L. Pressly, *The Life and Art of James Barry* (New Haven and London: Yale University Press, 1981) for a catalogue of Barry's prints.

25. Ellis Waterhouse, *Reynolds* (London: Kegan Paul, Trench Trubner and Co. Ltd., 1941), p. 134.

26. See Alexander, "The Dublin Group...," for more information about Irish mezzotinters living in London.

27. Griffiths, "Prints after Reynolds...," p. 44.

28. Ellis Waterhouse, *Painting in Britain, 1530-1790* (London and Baltimore: Penquin Books Ltd., 2nd ed., 1962), p. 211.

29. I am grateful to Nicholas Turner at the British Museum for this information.

30. K.T. Parker, *The Drawings of Hans Holbein in the Collection of His Majesty at Windsor Castle* (Oxford: Phaidon Press, Ltd., 1945), p. 20.

31. Ibid., p. 21.

32. Sir Robert Strange, *An Enquiry into the Rise and Establishment of the Royal Academy of Arts* (London: E. and C. Dilly, 1775).

33. W.S. Baker, *William Sharp, Engraver* (Philadelphia: Gebbie and Barne Publishing, 1875), p. 30.

34. Alexander and Godfrey, *Painters and Engraving*, p. 54.

35. Pye, *Patronage of British Art*, pp. 249-250.

36. Richard T. Godfrey, *Printmaking in Britain* (Oxford: Phaidon Press, 1978), p. 45.

37. Quoted in Winifred Friedman, *Boydell's Shakespeare Gallery* (New York and London: Garland Publishing Inc., 1976), p. 205.

38. Helmut van Erffa, "King Lear by Benjamin West," *Rhode Island School of Design Museum Notes* XLIII (December 1956): 7.

39. Baker, *William Sharp, Engraver*, p. 30.

40. *Farington Diary*, May 26, 1804, vol. 6, p. 2331.

41. Burnet, *Practical Essays...*, p. 138; Godfrey, *Printmaking in Britain*, p. 46.

42. Friedman, *Boydell's Shakespeare Gallery*, p. 222.

43. The Art Gallery of Ontario also owns an impression from a later 1805 edition.

44. The other was a Shakespearean subject, *Queen Katharine's Dream*.

45. Quoted in Tuer, *Bartolozzi and his Works*, p. 418.

46. Quoted in T.S.R. Boase, "Macklin and Bowyer," *Journal of the Warburg and Courtauld Institutes* XXVI (1963), p. 169.

47. David Hume's *The History of England* was first published in three volumes between 1754 and 1762.

48. Roy Strong, *And when did you last see your father? The Victorian Painter and British History* (London: Thames and Hudson, 1978), p. 21.

49. David Hume, *The History of England from the Invasion of Julius Caesar to the Revolution in 1688* (London: Printed by T. Bensley, Bolt-Court, Fleet Street, for Robert Bowyer, Pall Mall, 1806), p. 498.

50. *Cymon and Iphegenia* (sic) was also issued in colour. Ruth Bleackley, "William Wynne Ryland's Engravings," *The Connoisseur* XII (June 1905):110.

51. Lady V. Manners and Dr. G.C. Williamson, *Angelica Kauffman, R.A.* (New York: Hacker Brothers, 1976, first pub. 1924), p. 54.

52. An impression in the British Museum was published by F. Bartolozzi in 1787 and is printed in brown ink.

53. Tuer, *Bartolozzi and his Works*, p. 135.

54. Only two of the paintings can be traced today.

55. Webster, *Francis Wheatley*, p. 85.

56. Pressly, *The Life and Art of James Barry*, p. 123.

57. Barry to the Society of Arts, March 31, 1801. William Pressly published this information in his catalogue on Barry written for the Tate Gallery exhibition earlier this year. I am grateful to him for allowing me to consult the entry on the Society of Arts series before publication.

58. Martin Hardie, *Watercolour Painting in Britain*, vol. 1 (London: B.T. Batsford Ltd., 1966), pp. 97-98.

59. "Letters from Paul Sandby to John Clerk of Eldin," *Print Collector's Quarterly* XX (October 1933), pp. 362-3.

60. Suggested by Patrick Noon and confirmed by John Riely in recent correspondence.

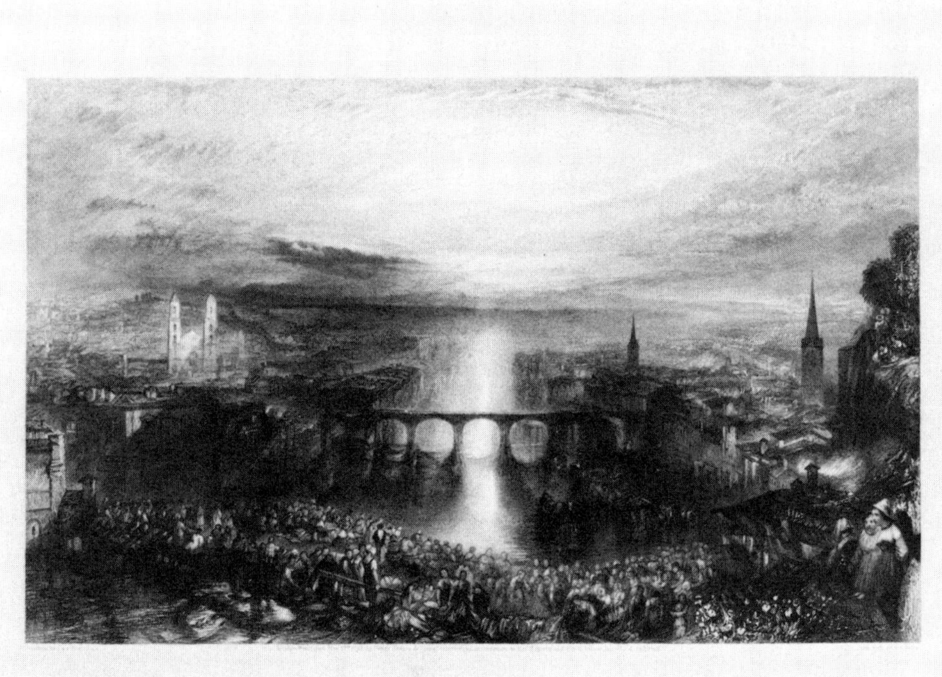

36. Prior after Turner, *Zurich,* 1854

The early nineteenth century

New Demands and New Markets

This is a distinction to which my art could in no case have arrived, confined from its nature to one place, were it not that it has been fortunately combined with yours, the excellence and beauty of which are wafted forth on a thousand wings and speak simultaneously to all countries and in all languages.

DAVID WILKIE TO ABRAHAM RAIMBACH, 1835[1]

WHEN THE "STORM OF THE FRENCH REVOLUTION BURST OVER THE different countries of Europe," it "suspended altogether the commerce by which British artists had been enabled to live."[2] Writing in 1845, the engraver John Pye emphasized the extent to which British art had come to depend upon foreign trade by the end of the previous century. Fortunately, the depressed state of the art market was temporary and the industrious British found new ways to survive at home in the meantime. The spread of literacy and the growth of a reading public by the 1780s had resulted in an increased demand for illustrated books. Abraham Raimbach (1766-1843), who would later become one of David Wilkie's principal engravers, was busy in the early nineteenth century with "book embellishments,"[3] and many other line-engravers found employment in book illustration schemes.

For at least three centuries line-engraving had been the most widely used process for illustration. From the 1780s to the 1830s, however, following its original introduction by Paul Sandby, aquatint became the preferred technique, particularly for landscape subjects. This fifty-year period was also the great age of landscape painting in watercolour, and some of the most popular images of the day were hand-coloured aquatints after watercolours, often of topographical subjects, issued singly or in books by publishers such as Rudolph Ackermann. Aquatints of sporting, military, and naval subjects also maintained a high level of success. The popularity of the technique was, nevertheless, shortlived.

By 1818 a new process, which could render the effects of drawings and watercolours with greater fidelity than any engraving technique, was firmly established in London. Lithography quickly supplanted both aquatint and stipple and was used extensively during the first half of the century for topographical landscapes. Few artists chose lithography, however, for reproductions of their works in oil. They preferred instead to remain loyal to the more prestigious intaglio techniques that were being continually modified and updated to meet the requirements of their paintings and to satisfy the demands of the marketplace.

J.M.W. TURNER

With the impact of the Industrial Revolution in Britain and the end of the continental wars by 1815, new markets for British engravings were opened up and painters endeavoured to take advantage of the potential dividends. J.M.W. Turner (1775-1851), for example, made several attempts to enter the lucrative market and spread his fame with prints after his heroic landscapes. Various printmakers executed line-engravings after his large watercolour and oil paintings (No. 36), and Turner provided drawings for steel-engraved book illustrations in popular annuals of the day, such as *The Keepsake.* It was, however, in the plates for his *Liber Studiorum* (1807-1819) and the *Little Liber* (c. 1825) that Turner became most personally involved in the engraving process.

In conceiving the *Liber Studiorum,* Turner was certainly aware of Claude Lorrain's *Liber Veritatis.* Claude's drawings had been engraved by Richard Earlom in mezzotint with etched outlines and published by Boydell in 1777. Turner was inspired by this series, as evidenced by his choice of the mezzotint technique, but unlike Earlom's interpretations, Turner wanted to go beyond a simple recording of specific drawings for posterity. He hoped rather to proclaim through the prints his complete mastery over all categories of landscape painting. He issued the series in parts with each part containing examples of several kinds of landscape, including Historical, Mountainous, Pastoral, Marine, and Architectural. The prints thus provide "a sort of check-list of the various kinds of art at which he had tried his hand."[4]

Turner etched his own plates but usually hired skilful engravers such as Charles Turner (1774-1857) for the application of the mezzotint (no. 34). In this way, he hoped to capture the brilliant lights and deep shadows that make his works in all media so dramatic. He nevertheless recognized that the engravings would not be mere copies of his drawings, but translations, and therefore works of art in their own right. Turner is quoted as saying that "Engrav(ing) is or ought to be a translation of a Picture, for the nature of each art varies so much in the means of expressing the same objects that lines become the language of colours."[5]

Although Turner appreciated the artistic value of the engravings, his aim for the entire series was at the same time extremely practical, because he desired "more profit than a painter normally received from engravings after his work."[6] Pragmatism was a hallmark of the nineteenth century, and Turner's attitude was also shared by other artists who were becoming keenly aware of the value of the print.

John Martin

One such contemporary was John Martin (1789-1854), who is known to have made £21,000 between 1826 and 1840 in royalties and the direct sale of prints after his paintings.[7] Martin's paintings of apocalyptic visions were greatly admired when they were first exhibited, and the tiny, brightly painted figures, overwhelmed by vast cavernous spaces, translated well into mezzotint. When steel plates were introduced in the 1820s Martin capitalized on the promise of ever larger editions brought by this harder surface.

Martin published huge engravings at regular intervals for over ten years, and also designed and engraved for fashionable annuals, including *The Forget-me-not, The Keepsake, The Amulet,* and *The Iris.* Some of his best-known prints were his illustrations to Milton's *Paradise Lost.* He worked on the series from 1825 to 1827, completing two sets of twenty-four prints, a large and a small series of the same subjects (nos. 37 and 38). Although these works are not strictly reproductive because Martin designed and engraved the subjects entirely on the plate and they are not related to specific paintings, they typify his approach to all his mezzotint projects. Skilfully manipulating the velvety blacks and brilliant whites of the process, Martin invented other-worldly creatures radiating with the light of heaven or the flames of hell, enveloped in deep dark expanses.

John Constable

In contrast to the mystical visions of Martin, John Constable (1776-1837) preferred quieter views of familiar landscapes. First in 1830 and again in 1833, he published in book form with accompanying letter-press a series of twenty-two mezzotints, which reproduced mostly out-of-door oil sketches. The series did not bring him the acclaim or financial dividends he desired because, like the paintings, the engravings were spontaneous records of nature and were similarly ahead of their time. Although Constable chose the mezzotint technique apparently in response to Turner's prints, he once called the Turner series the "Liber Stupidorum," emphasizing the different aims of the two painters.[8] While Turner captured grand, generalized views of nature, Constable recorded the climatic conditions and atmospheric changes of specific locations by analysing "the day, the hour, the sunshine, and the shade."[9]

He did not personally engrave the plates for the *Various Subjects of Landscape Characteristic of English Scenery,* but found in the mezzotint engraver David Lucas (1802-1881) a very sympathetic interpreter, who became almost an extension of his own mind and hand. Lucas' ability to translate Constable's unique and fresh approach to nature is admirably illustrated by *Spring* (No. 39) and *Hadleigh Castle, Near the Nore* (No. 40). Recognizing Lucas' special sensitivity to his oil sketches and his ability as an artist, Constable wrote to the engraver, 'I shall never have a doubt...of the sincerity of your love for my things in landscape....We have a bond of friendship...a unison of feeling in art and...in the lovely amalgamation of our works."[10]

Portraits

Along with the landscapes of Constable and Turner, and the supernatural subjects of Martin, the portrait mezzotint was still very much alive and well in the 1820s and 1830s. Reynolds' paintings continued to be engraved, and mezzotints after the portraits of the contemporary painter Sir Thomas Lawrence (1769-1830) also became great favourites. Samuel Cousins (1801-1887), for example, who became an important engraver of Victorian paintings (nos. 58-61), made his name in the 1820s by engraving thirty-three works after Lawrence.[11]

Lawrence's attitude to the sale of prints after his paintings places him squarely in the nineteenth century. Whereas in the previous century copyrights to paintings were sold by the owner of the painting or occasionally by the painter to an engraver or publisher for very small sums, painters such as Lawrence recognized the potential value of the copyright. It became possible by the 1820s for an artist to sell the painting and the copyright as independent commodities for almost equal amounts of money.[12]

David wilkie

David Wilkie (1785-1841), who was noted for his tenacious promotion of engravings after his paintings among printsellers, was quick to take advantage of this new copyright arrangement. In 1822 he scored an overwhelming success at the Royal Academy when he exhibited *Chelsea Pensioners Reading the Gazette.* Soon after the Duke of Wellington paid the artist £1260 for the painting and, capitalizing on the popularity of the image, Wilkie sold the copyright for £1100 to the engraver John Burnet (1784-1868)and the publishers Boys and Graves.[13]

Wilkie's narrative genre themes could not have appeared at a more opportune time. The new middle-class art audience saw themselves mirrored in these scenes in the same way that their lives were reflected in current novels by Sir Walter Scott. In subjects such as *Chelsea Pensioners* and *Distraining for Rent,* engraved by Abraham Raimbach (1766-1843) and published in 1828 (No. 42), everyday experiences were chronicled, and although sentimentalized, nevertheless rang true-to-life. Later in the century, Sir Edwin Landseer (1802-1873), Thomas Faed (1826-1900) and William Powell Frith (1819-1909) would overshadow Wilkie, by painting similar but even more anecdotal subjects, and reaching a much bigger popular audience through engraved interpretations of their paintings.

Curiously, Wilkie and his principal engravers, Burnet and Raimbach, maintained a traditional eighteenth-century attitude to technique, rejecting mezzotint and stipple because of their supposed inferiority to line-engraving. All prints after Wilkie were made using the elaborate system of lines and cross-hatchings that were distinctive to line-engraving on copper, and as such represent almost the last vestiges of a great technique that was to be little used after 1830. With the introduction of steel plates and other technical innovations, line-engraving became too slow and laborious. During the rest of the nineteenth century few techniques were used in their traditional or pure forms, but were altered and combined to accomodate the clamouring of the printsellers and the public for "Victorian engravings."

32. THOMAS ROWLANDSON (British, 1756-1827)

Imposition c.1812-14
Pencil, pen, and watercolour on wove paper
27.5 x 21.6 cm
Inscribed in ink at lower centre margin: Imposition
Purchase, 1937
Acc. no. 2453

33. THOMAS ROWLANDSON (British, 1756-1827)
after his own watercolour

Miseries of London or Surly Saucy Hackney Coachman 1814
Hand-coloured etching on wove paper
33.0 x 23.5 cm (sheet)
Gift of the Trier-Fodor Foundation, 1978
Acc. no. 78/110

Many caricatures fall into the general category of reproductive prints because they are made after original watercolours and drawings. Rowlandson was a talented draughtsman and a very subtle colourist who is best known for his social caricatures. He also took a keen interest in the duplication of his images, often etching his own plates.

The exact relationship between the *Miseries of London* impression and the *Imposition* watercolour has not been determined, although the images are very closely linked.[14] Several discrepancies between the two works suggest that perhaps the etching was made by a professional printmaker after Rowlandson's design, rather than by Rowlandson himself.[15] Small details of the setting have been altered, but even more obvious are several changes to the figures and to the horse. An illogical third leg has been added to the two legs of the horse visible in the watercolour. The servant girl in the doorway has been given a body that is too large in proportion to the size of her head. She also carries a candle, making the daylight of the watercolour into a night scene.

The etching was hand-coloured in bright hues that bear no relationship to the subdued colours of *Imposition*, but are typical of the Thomas Tegg workshop, which issued many of Rowlandson's prints. Colouring by the assembly-line method was commonly used for caricatures.

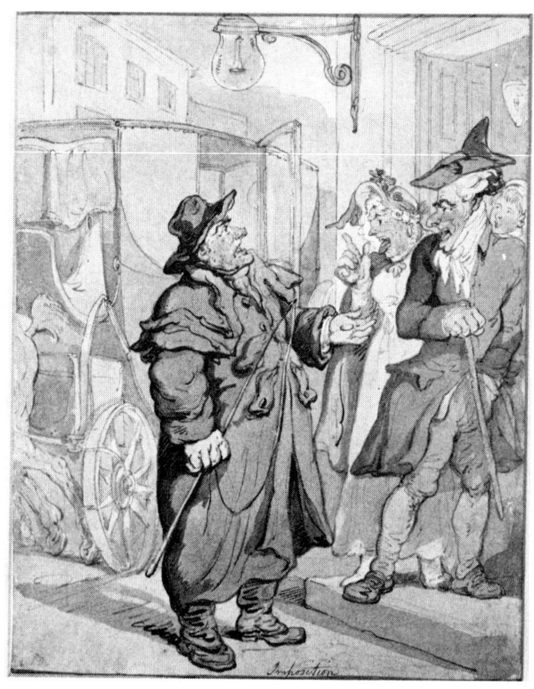

32. Rowlandson, *Imposition*, c. 1815

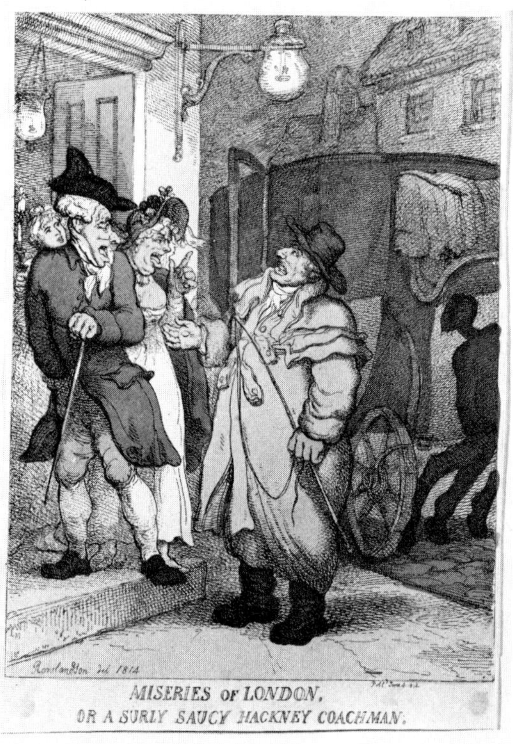

33. Rowlandson, *Miseries of London*, 1814

J.M.W. TURNER'S LANDSCAPES

34. JOHN MALLORD WILLIAM TURNER (British, 1775-1851) and CHARLES TURNER (British, 1774-1857)

Pembury Mill, Kent from the *Liber Studiorum*
1808 R.12 I/3
Etching and mezzotint in sepia on wove paper
20.3 x 29.1 cm (imp.)
Purchase, 1927
Acc. no. 1169

35. JOHN MALLORD WILLIAM TURNER (British, 1775-1851) and WILLIAM SAY (British, 1768-1834)

Tenth Plague of Egypt from the *Liber Studiorum*
1816 R.61 I/3
Etching and mezzotint in sepia on wove paper
21.3 x 29.1 cm
Purchase, 1927
Acc. no. 1175

Turner received acclaim for his paintings very early in his career. In 1799 at the age of twenty-four, he was elected Associate of the Royal Academy and three years later became a full Academician. The seventy-one *Liber Studiorum* engravings, published in fourteen parts between 1807 and 1819, demonstrated his expertise in rendering all the various styles of landscape that were valued by artists historically, and provided an overview of the categories of landscape painting at which he had tried his hand. *Pembury Mill,* for example, was classified as a "Pastoral" subject while the *Tenth Plague of Egypt* is representative of the "Historical" category.

Turner etched the plates himself but employed professional engravers for the mezzotinting process. Whatever the media of the original work, whether an oil, watercolour, or a monochrome sketch, he provided his engravers with highly finished sepia drawings, which were executed in pen and brown wash with white highlights, to use as models.[16] He carefully supervised the work to assure that the tonal areas were as rich and subtle as in his drawings and that the white, scraped accents were as dramatic. Charles Turner (see also No. 4) mezzotinted the first twenty plates of the series before an argument over his remuneration ended his employment.

36. THOMAS ABEL PRIOR (British, 1809-1886) after J.M.W. TURNER (British, 1775-1851)

Zurich 1854 R.672
Line-engraving and etching on india paper
42.2 x 62.2 cm (imp.)
Gift of F.M. Kimbark
Acc. no. 81/529
Printsellers' Association stamp: YKV

Zurich was one of ten Swiss views that Turner painted in watercolour in 1845. The original is now in the Kunsthaus, Zurich, and is known as *Zurich: fête, early morning.* Andrew Wilton has described the work as Turner's "most ecstatic account of urban life, a life that revolves round a vortex of glistening water, radiant sky and distant mountains."[17] Thomas A. Prior engraved this plate after the painter's death, but has managed to convey something of the light and air of Turner's original watercolour. The closeness and fineness of the lines are characteristic of mid-nineteenth-century steel engraving.

MEZZOTINTS AFTER JOHN MARTIN AND JOHN CONSTABLE

JOHN MARTIN (British, 1789-1854) after his own design

37. *Satan Tempting Eve* from Milton's *Paradise Lost*
Bk. 9 line 780 1827
Proof before letters
Mezzotint on laid paper
19.4 x 27.8 cm (image)
Gift of Touche Ross, 1980
Acc. no. 80/54

38. *Bridge over Chaos* from Milton's *Paradise Lost*
Bk.10 lines 312 and 347 1827
Proof before letters
Mezzotint on wove paper
25.5 x 34.5 cm (imp.)
Gift of Inco Limited, 1981
Acc. no. 79/19

From the mid-1820s to the late 1830s John Martin's spectacular canvases were great favourites with the general public, second only to Turner's epic paintings. His popularity was largely achieved and maintained through the issuing of reproductive prints, which also provided him with a major source of income. Prior to the mid-1820s, Martin's first-hand experience with printmaking was confined to a few small etchings and experiments in mezzotint. His commission in 1823 to engrave illustrations for Milton's *Paradise Lost* launched his career

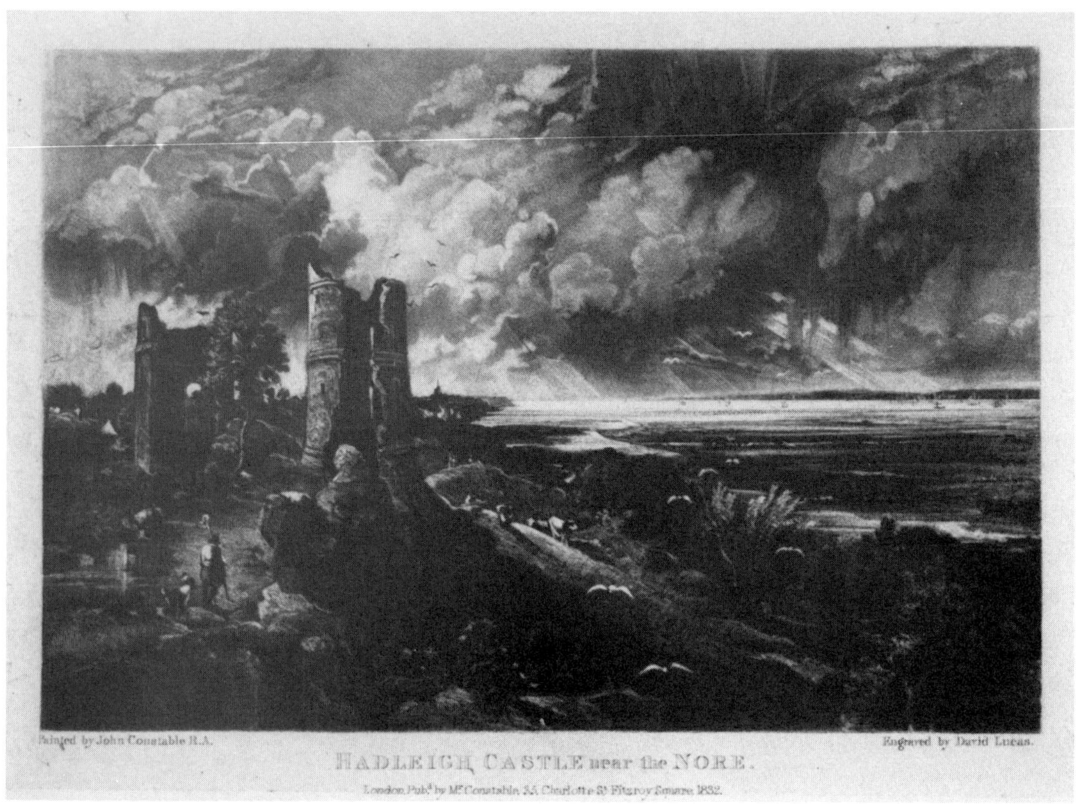

40. Lucas after Constable, *Hadleigh Castle near the Nore*, 1832

as a printmaker, and led to the making of a series, during the next fifteen years, of large plates after his canvases. These works were executed by Martin himself, or by others under his close supervision.

Martin was paid £2000 by the publisher Septimus Prowett for the set of twenty-four plates illustrating Milton (nos. 37 and 38), and £1500 for a second set that reduced the same images to a smaller size. Both sets were published between 1825 and 1827. These and Martin's subsequent engravings took advantage of the newly introduced steel plates, which could be printed in almost unlimited editions, guaranteeing Martin's wide exposure. The *Paradise Lost* series was for the most part worked out entirely on the plates, so that although Martin made preliminary oil sketches for each mezzotint,[18] the works are more correctly called "original" rather than "reproductive." They are nevertheless representative of Martin's later engravings, both in terms of imagery and technique.

Mezzotint was well-suited to Martin's apocalyptic visions. Working from dark to light as dictated by the technique, the artist allowed the velvety black to remain as the awful nothingness that engulfs the tiny, brightly scraped figures. His representations of Hell and Satan are particularly effective and dramatic. The tunnel-shaped form in the *Bridge over Chaos* (No. 38) has been linked to contemporary illustrations of the Thames Tunnel, first opened to the public in 1827.[19]

39. DAVID LUCAS (British, 1802-1881)
after JOHN CONSTABLE (British, 1776-1837)

Spring 1830 S.7 II/5
Mezzotint on laid paper
15.5 x 25.5 cm (imp.)
Gift of Mr. and Mrs. Ralph Presgrave, 1978
Acc. no. 78/58

40. *Hadleigh Castle near the Nore* 1832 S.34 I/4
Mezzotint on india paper
18.0 x 25.3 cm (imp.)
Purchase, 1982
Acc. no. 81/275

In 1830 Constable published a series of twenty-two mezzotints after his landscape paintings. Three years later he issued the second edition under the title *Various Subjects of Landscape, characteristic of English Scenery, principally intended to mark the Phenomena of the Chiar'Oscuro of Nature.* The series, financed by the painter, represents his only attempt to publicize his works in oil through engravings. Unfortunately, the venture was not a monetary success.

The obvious prototype for Constable's series was Turner's *Liber Studiorum* as suggested by his choice of the mezzotint technique, and by his attempt to provide a kind of checklist of his works in oil. His aim was not, however, to produce grand, historical landscapes, but "to promote the study of the Rural Scenery of England" and to capture the "effects of light and shadow upon landscape." He emphasized that only "real places" and direct "transcripts" of nature as actually observed were worthy of inclusion.[20]

The vigorous brushwork and somber, stormy moods of Constable's late period were particularly suited to the mezzotint technique. David Lucas had been trained by the well known engraver S.W. Reynolds (1774-1835) and became a very sympathetic interpreter of the painter's transient skies and dramatic lighting effects. By the 1830s mezzotint was most often used in combination with other techniques, particularly etching, making Lucas' plates some of the last examples in the early nineteenth century of the pure mezzotint technique. Like Turner, Constable was intimately involved in the printmaking process, giving Lucas many verbal and written instructions and correcting endless proofs. Unlike Turner's engravers, however, Lucas did not have elaborate sepia drawings to use as models but worked from small oil sketches, "direct records of nature" such as *Spring* (c. 1816), now in the Victoria and Albert Museum; or occasionally from larger oil paintings such as *Hadleigh Castle, Mouth of the Thames – Morning after a Stormy Night,* exhibited at the Royal Academy in 1829 and now at the Yale Center for British Art.

ENGRAVINGS AFTER DAVID WILKIE'S GENRE PAINTINGS

ABRAHAM RAIMBACH (British, 1766-1843)
after DAVID WILKIE (British, 1785-1841)

41. *Distraining for Rent* 1824
Etching on india paper
51.0 x 66.0 cm (imp.)
Purchase, 1981
Acc. no. 81/101

42. *Distraining for Rent* 1828
Line-engraving and etching on india paper
51.0 x 66.0 cm (imp.)
Purchase, 1982

David Wilkie's *Distraining for Rent* was exhibited at the Royal Academy in 1815 and now forms part of the collection of the National Gallery of Scotland, Edinburgh. Influenced by seventeenth-century Dutch and Flemish genre painting, Wilkie's narrative subjects were popular throughout the early nineteenth century. Engravings after his paintings were also best-sellers and largely responsible for diffusing his fame. Although Wilkie etched a few original plates, his primary involvement with printmaking was through the reproductive prints made by professional engravers after his paintings. One of his principal engravers, Abraham Raimbach, executed a series of large plates after the painter beginning in 1812. Until that time most of Raimbach's line-engravings had been small-scale book illustrations. He welcomed the opportunity to work on a larger scale and "escape the thraldom" of devoting all his labours to "their being shut up in a book."[21] Wilkie and Raimbach enjoyed a very amicable arrangement, whereby the engraver owned three-quarters of the copyright to the plates while the painter owned one-quarter.

The inspiration for *Distraining for Rent* apparently came from Wilkie's personal experience. According to Raimbach, in 1812 several of the painter's canvases had been seized in lieu of rent payments and this led to "the production of one of his pictures of the highest degree of excellence, namely Distraining for Rent, which he commenced immediately afterwards."[22] Raimbach insisted that the subject would make a successful engraving, although "Mr. Wilkie, with his never-failing sagacity, doubted from the first of the prudence of the undertaking, on the score of its melancholy subject, and waived his objections in compliance with my earnestly expressed wishes."[23]

The extensive preliminary etching of the plate was completed in 1824 (No. 41), but Raimbach did not begin the line-engraving until late in 1825. The work was finally published by the painter and the engraver in 1828. Sales of the engraving languished, and it became one of their least successful ventures. The engraver concluded that the "distressful nature" of the subject, as well as Wilkie's diminishing fame after twenty years of "extreme popularity," were both partly responsible.[24]

ANDREAS J. FLEISCHMANN (German, 1811-1878)
after DAVID WILKIE (British, 1785-1841)

43. *Die Auspfändung (Distraining for Rent)* 1846-7
Line-engraving, proof impression on wove paper
33.0 x 40.0 cm (imp.)
Purchase, 1981
Acc. no. 81/100.1

44. *Die Auspfändung (Distraining for Rent)* 1846-7
Line-engraving on wove paper
33.0 x 40.0 cm (imp.)
Purchase, 1981
Acc. no. 81/100.6

Published in Germany eighteen years after Raimbach's publication in England, Fleischmann's engraving emphasizes that Wilkie's images were recognized and in demand on the continent. In addition, it stresses the close ties between England and Germany, particularly in the years following Queen Victoria's marriage to Prince Albert in 1840.

NOTES

1. M.T.S. Raimbach, *Memoirs and Recollections of the late Abraham Raimbach* (London: Frederick Shoberl, 1843), p. 128. A letter from Wilkie to Raimbach when they became members of the Academy of Fine Arts in the French Institute, December, 1835.

2. John Pye, *Patronage of British Art* (London: Longman, Brown, Green and Longmans, 1845), pp. 252-253.

3. Ibid., p. 372.

4. Andrew Wilton, *Turner and the Sublime* (London: British Museum Publications, 1980), p. 69.

5. Quoted in John Gage, *Colour in Turner* (London: Studio Vista Ltd., 1969), p. 51.

6. Richard T. Godfrey, *Printmaking in Britain* (Oxford; Phaidon Press, 1978), p. 82. For example, see W.G. Rawlinson, *The Engraved Work of J.M.W. Turner, R.A.*, vol. 1 (London: Macmillan and Co., Ltd.), pp. 34-35.

7. Mary L. Pendered, *John Martin, Painter: His Life and Times* (New York: E.P. Dutton and Co., 1924), p. 162.

8. Noted in Andrew Wilton, *Constable's 'English Landscape Scenery'* (London: British Museum Publications, 1979), p. 9.

9. Introduction to the second edition of Constable's *English Landscape Scenery*, 1833. In Wilton, *Constable's 'English Landscape Scenery*,' p. 24.

10. R.B. Beckett, *John Constable's Correspondence*, vol. 4 (Suffolk Records Society, 1966), p. 416. Letter to Lucas, December, 1834.

11. Alfred Whitman, *Nineteenth Century Mezzotinters: Samuel Cousins, R.A.* (London: George Bell, 1904), p. 15.

12. David Alexander and Richard T. Godfrey, *Painters and Engraving: The Reproductive Print from Hogarth to Wilkie* (New Haven: Yale Center for British Art, 1980), pp. 12, 69.

13. Noted in Alexander and Godfrey, pp. 70-71.

14. See Katharine Jordan Lochnan, *Selected Impressions: Recent Acquisitions of Master Prints from the Fifteenth to the Twentieth Century* (Toronto: Art Gallery of Ontario, 1979), p. 30.

15. Suggested by Patrick Noon and confirmed by John Riely in recent correspondence. Mr. Riely also tentatively dated the watercolour to c. 1812-14.

16. The drawings are now in the British Museum.

17. Wilton, *Turner and the Sublime*, p. 171.

18. William Feaver, *The Art of John Martin* (Oxford: Clarendon Press, 1975), p. 75. The entire series of oil sketches was sold by Sotheby's in March, 1964.

19. F.D. Klingender, *Art and the Industrial Revolution* (London: Evelyn, Adams and MacKay, 1968), p. 123.

20. Introduction to the second edition of Constable's *English Landscape Scenery*, 1833. In Wilton, *Constable's 'English Landscape Scenery*,' p. 24.

21. Raimbach, *Memoirs*, p. 112.

22. Raimbach, *Memoirs*, pp. 113-114.

23. Raimbach, *Memoirs*, p. 123.

24. Raimbach, *Memoirs*, p. 134.

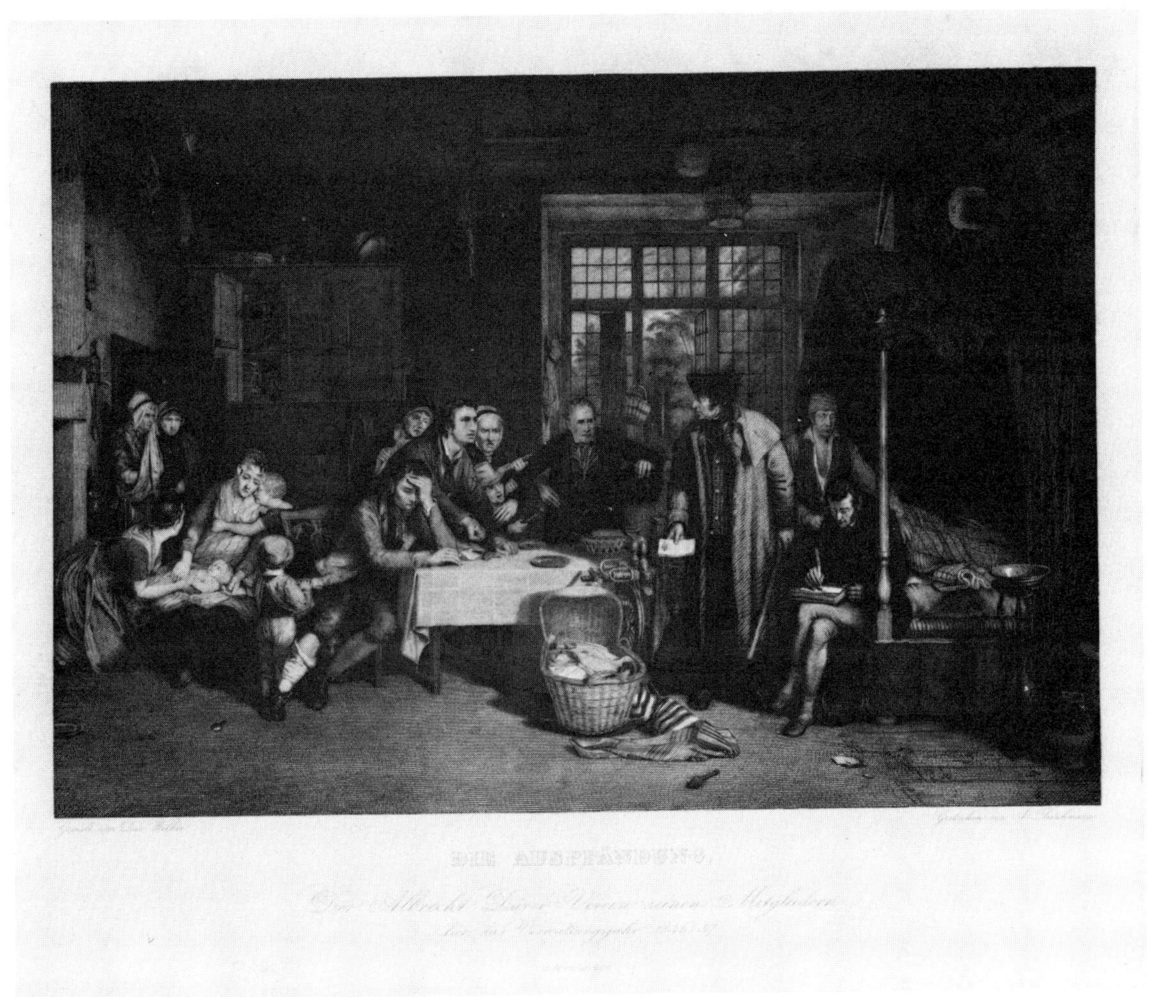

44. Fleischmann after Wilkie, *Die Auspfändung (Distraining for Rent)*, 1846-7

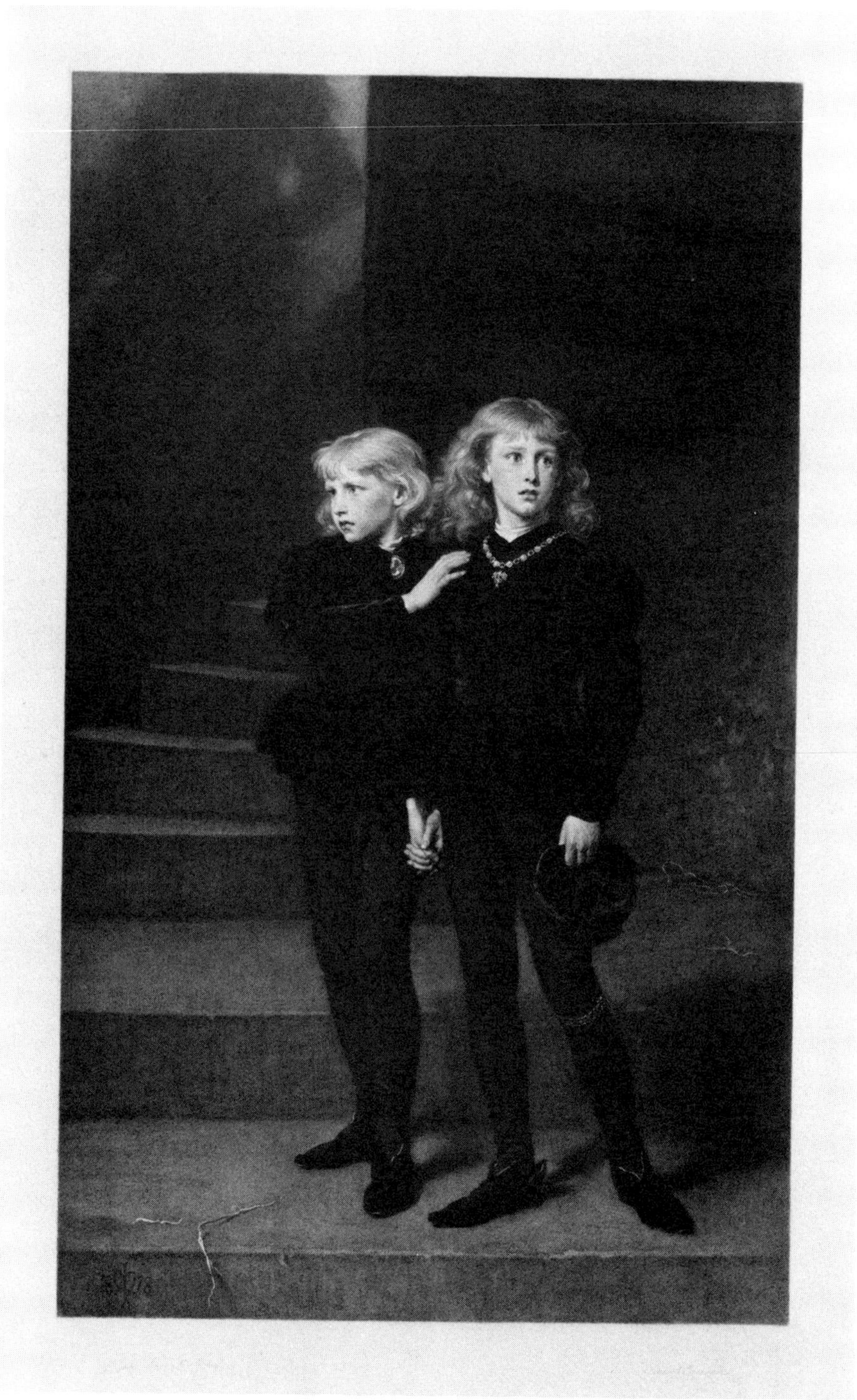

61. Cousins after Millais, *The Princes in the Tower,* 1879

The Victorian Era and the Truly Popular Print

Indeed a national service is rendered by the publication of really noble transcripts from noble pictures like these. Where the picture cannot go, the engravings penetrate.

F. G. STEPHENS ON ENGRAVINGS
AFTER WILLIAM HOLMAN HUNT'S PAINTINGS, 1860[1]

THE REIGN OF QUEEN VICTORIA COINCIDED WITH A PERIOD OF ENORMOUS growth and development in many areas of human endeavour. It was an age of industry and travel, with the railway and the steamship bringing the possibility of vast world markets. As well as providing the technological know-how to accommodate new markets, the Industrial Revolution also encouraged the growth of a literate, moneyed and art-interested middle class. Municipal galleries were opened and a continuous run of public exhibitions was highlighted by the Great Exhibition in 1851 and the Manchester Art Treasures Exhibition in 1857. Art, for the first time, became a primary source of entertainment and edification for the majority of the populace.

The print business was also booming as a result. To satisfy demand, unlimited quantities and ever more accurate copies became the goals of the print publishers, many of whom amassed large fortunes. Painters also maintained high incomes through the sale of reproduction rights, which sometimes proved more lucrative than the sale of their paintings. As early as the 1840s Edwin Landseer (nos. 50, 51) annually made several thousand pounds from his paintings and netted at least that much again from copyrights.[2]

In contrast, in the words of an eye-witness, the lives of most Victorian printmakers were characterized by "great toil" and they "earned their money slowly."[3] Just as their counterparts in the eighteenth century had suffered from lack of respect, they were often considered to be skilled but inferior workmen. To some extent, however, such labels were justified;

as engraving styles became more homogeneous, the unique hand of the individual became less apparent. One recent scholar has described the Victorian engraver as an "artisan whose personality was entirely excluded by the mechanics of his trade,"[4] and as early as 1866, the etcher Seymour Haden (1818-1910) denounced the reproductive print, calling it "wholly, or almost wholly, mechanical."[5] The engraver's hard work to make ever more perfect copies resulted in his own anonymity and the eventual loss of the job to photographic processes. His ultimate redundancy was precipitated by a widespread demand for all kinds of reproductive prints.

From sixpenny pictures sold by the street-corner hawker to elaborately framed "artist-proof" engravings available from more elegant establishments, prints of popular paintings became a distinctly Victorian feature of everyday life. By the 1860s even the lower middle class could afford a "two guinea proof in a five shilling frame."[6] No parlour was without a display of framed pictures, which were largely dominated by interior figural scenes that reflected the lives and morals of Victorian society.

George Baxter and Colour Printing

Many parlours numbered among their wall decorations the small oil-colour prints of George Baxter (1804-1867) (No. 45). Contemporary paintings provided the models for many of Baxter's works, but he often designed his own images. A typical Baxter print employed one lithographic stone or one intaglio plate with up to thirty colour wood blocks. As well as wall prints, these works were often pasted onto boxes or into ladies' scrapbooks as decorations.

Baxter's method was one of a number of colour-printing processes developed during the period. Supplements in the *Illustrated London News,* which appeared regularly and reproduced contemporary paintings, were cheaply printed in colour using a method related to Baxter's.[7] They could be removed from the publication and framed to hang on the wall. Chromolithography, which required a separate lithographic stones for each colour, was another popular process. Some of the best chromolithographs were the series after Old Master paintings sponsored by the Arundel Society beginning in the 1850s, which were intended to educate and elevate the masses. Various other colour intaglio and relief processes were used primarily for book illustration.[8]

Black-and-White Illustration

More leisure time and the desire to be surrounded by art fostered a variety of publications and new printing methods to accomodate them. In the field of periodical illustration, two black-and-white techniques, steel engraving and wood engraving, were dominant at least until the 1870s. The introduction of steel plates by the 1820s and the invention of stereotyping and electrotyping (both of which involved making moulds and, in essence, duplicating the original plate or wood block) assured the feasibility and popularity of the two processes.

Throughout the history of engraving, copper had been used almost exclusively as an engraving surface. Although some copper plates yielded more, a thousand impressions was usually maximum for line-engraving or etching, and considerably fewer for mezzotint. In 1822 Thomas Lupton (1791-1873) introduced the first steel plate. This harder metal could produce 15,000 or more impressions. Steel plates were used extensively to illustrate novels, poetry, and particularly the early annuals such as *The Keepsake* and *The Book of Beauty.* Among the more eminent artists providing designs for the annuals were J.M.W. Turner (1775-1851) and John Martin (1789-1854). Arthur Hayden, writing in 1906, had an amusing explanation for the popularity of the annuals:

> The early Victorian drawing-room was another factor in the problem. Our forbears loved to decorate their drawing-room tables with a series of sumptuous volumes arranged as the spokes of a cart-wheel. The "Keepsake," the "Book of Beauty," and others of a similar character, embellished with minute steel engravings, were produced to supply this demand.[2]

A typical steel engraving combined etching and line-engraving using an essentially linear approach. Its distinctive appearance is apparent in Thomas A. Prior's (1809-1886) *Zurich* after J.M.W. Turner (No. 36). Because of the hardness of the metal, the resulting impression is a highly finished, detailed image, with very closely laid grey, rather than dark black, lines and an overall lack of the richness found in prints from copper plates.

The relief technique wood engraving was in competition for the same audience, but its advantage over steel engraving and lithography was that text and illustration could be printed together. Unlike the woodcut, wood engraving was made using the hard-grain end of the wood, and was usually characterized by fine white lines on a black background (No. 47), although the reverse can be true (No. 46).

John Everett Millais (1829-1896), William Holman Hunt (1827-1910), and many other High Victorian painters provided drawings for well known wood engraving firms such as W.J. Linton, Joseph Swain, and the Dalziel brothers. The drawings were mounted or drawn directly onto wood blocks and they were therefore destroyed in the engraving process. By the mid-1860s, photographs of the originals could be mounted onto the blocks so that the drawings were preserved.

The 1860s represents the great age of black-and-white illustration, when wood engraving flourished in periodicals such as *Once a Week, Good Words,* and *The Cornhill Magazine.* Millais' drawings for the publication *The Parables of Our Lord* are particularly well reproduced in white-line wood engravings that capture the sensitivity and precision of the originals (No. 47).

Mixed-Method Engraving

The most prestigious prints of the Victorian period were the large, singly issued engravings after popular contemporary paintings; prints that could be elaborately framed as wall decorations. Such works, however, were more than ornamental; they were "Books, . . . Histories and Sermons,"[10] combining just enough anecdote and sobriety to appeal to popular taste. They entertained the viewer but often chastized and reminded him at the same time of the ideals of patriotism, heroism, or upright Christian conduct.

Very few painters reproduced their own paintings during the Victorian period, leaving the task to skilled "artisan" engravers. Notable exceptions were the remarkable engraving by James Sharples (1825-1892) called *The Forge*, John Linnell's (1792-1882) many prints after his own canvases (No. 48), and the various etchings of James Tissot (1836-1902) after his paintings of modern urban life (No. 68).[11]

Line-engraving also declined during the period, because new methods seemed more suited to steel plates. The favoured technique for reproduction of Victorian paintings was the mixed method or mixed style and - since the predominant process was often mezzotint - mixed mezzotint. The mixed method could combine as many as four or five intaglio processes on one plate, including mezzotint, etching, stipple, aquatint, line-engraving, and drypoint.

Mixed techniques were certainly not unknown in the eighteenth century, when combinations of etching and line-engraving or etching and stipple were in common usage. The only prints that remained essentially pure were portrait mezzotints. By the turn of the century this practice was also revised, with combinations of etching and mezzotint even in portrait reproductions (No. 4). Such techniques were employed for several reasons. Apart from speed, perhaps the most important was the desire to copy or approximate the original medium, whether it was oil, watercolour, or chalk. Similarly, Victorian engravings continued the tradition of accurately approximating their models.

The glossy surface and the detailed, less painterly approach of many painters, epitomized by Pre-Raphaelite works of the 1850s and 1860s,was translated by a comparable high polish and an accumulation of tiny lines and dots on the plate. The Victorians' love for detail was evident in all aspects of life, from the books they read to the way they decorated their homes. In art, detail implied realism and authenticity and was also a sign of hard work and a measure of the length of time spent. It is therefore not surprising that large steel engravings were very elaborately finished.

Through an increasingly sophisticated approach to the plate, engravings became virtuoso technical achievements, but with very little to distinguish one engraver's hand from another. Devices such as the ruling machine, invented by Wilson Lowry (1762-1824) in 1790 and improved in 1798, were used to fill in large areas of the plate, particularly the background, with monotonous but regular lines and dots.[12] This "mechanical" approach to printmaking persisted and flourished because it helped to satisfy the desires of the public for large numbers of very accurate copies produced in record time.

Sir Edwin Landseer and Narrative Subjects

The paintings of Sir Edwin Landseer (1802-1873) were often interpreted by means of mixed-method engraving. Landseer's subjects were the direct descendents of David Wilkie's anecdotal genre scenes, but by the 1850s Landseer had overshadowed Wilkie, tapping the new urban market for overtly sentimental rustic scenes. Landseer has been called the "supreme example of the copyright artist" because he owed much of his fame and his financial success to his exposure through engravings. A Landseer painting was not merely a "finished product,...[but] essentially a stage in the sequence of events from inception to acceptance by a nation-wide, even a world-wide, public."[13]

His animal subjects had particular appeal, and one of the most striking and famous images of the period was Landseer's portrayal of a proud stag, *The Monarch of the Glen.* It was engraved by his brother Thomas Landseer (1795-1880) in 1852. Two other animal engravings after Landseer enjoyed almost equal celebrity. *The Old Shepherd's Chief Mourner* and *The Shepherd's Grave* (nos. 50 and 51) were engraved using the mixed-mezzotint technique by Frederick Hollyer (fl. 1860s) in 1868. The pictures describe the forlorn state of a sheepdog after the death of his master, and are vivid demonstrations of two themes that often recur in mid-Victorian painting - a fascination with death and the extensive use of anthropomorphism. In the words of one writer, animals "were even more capable of expressing their emotions without reserve, of being human without vulgarity. With them Landseer became the most popular and typical painter of the period."[14]

Apart from animals, Victorians also appreciated the anecdote and narrative provided by themes from current novels, Shakespeare, and Milton (No. 57), subjects from British history (No. 61), and Biblical themes (nos. 48 and 49). Other popular engravings highlighted current events and real-life situations (No. 52). Women were often featured as the heroines of the stories, illustrated by Millais' series *Yes or No?*, *No!* and *Yes!* (nos. 58-60). This sequence documents the progressive responses of a young woman confronted with the question of marriage. The story was presented to the public in instalments, just as contemporary novels were published in parts. This method of presentation, along with the apparent addition by Millais of the third panel *Yes!* in 1877 after public outcry over *No!* in 1875, emphasizes that Victorian pictures were meant to be entertaining, and that viewer response and involvement was expected.

Millais, like Landseer, owed a great debt to engraving. His paintings were among the most frequently engraved of the Victorian period and contributed significantly to his income of £25,000 to £40,000 a year![15] One of his principal engravers was Samuel Cousins (1801-1887), a man much admired for his highly polished mezzotint technique, and almost the only nineteenth-century reproductive engraver who has earned enough acclaim to have a substantial biography written about him![16]

Cousins was also responsible for one of the most sober and successful engravings of the mid-Victorian period. In 1860, Henry Graves published *The Mitherless Bairn* after Thomas Faed (1826-1900) (No. 53). Following, as had Landseer, in Wilkie's footsteps, Faed's works appealed to the current taste for genre themes. Rural life, in contrast to the grime of the city, was romantically viewed as idyllic and is shown here as a safe refuge for an orphaned street urchin. The subject had particular poignancy given the high rate of maternal deaths in childbirth during the period, and this scene of stable domesticity was sure to appeal to contemporary audiences.

Victorian family life also revolved around religion and Biblical engravings were much in demand, particularly those after William Holman Hunt. The print publisher Ernest Gambart purchased the copyright to one of the best known of all Victorian paintings, *The Light of the World* by Hunt, and published the engraving by William Henry Simmons (1811-1882) in 1860. Simmons was a very gifted and prolific engraver, executing works in both the mixed-mezzotint technique and in combinations of etching and aquatint with stipple (nos. 52, 55 and 56). *The Light of the World* became Simmons' most successful engraving, the most popular that Gambart ever published, and the one most frequently pirated![17]

Printsellers and Publishers

Gambart and his fellow print dealers in London were instrumental in bringing the demand for reproductive prints to a peak by the 1870s. At the time of Hogarth, twelve printsellers' shops carried on business in London,[18] while a hundred years later in 1839 Pigot's *Directory* recorded seventy-two printsellers and print publishers,[19] and by the 1880s approximately 125 such establishments were listed with the Printsellers' Association. Some of the most renowned during the Victorian period were Rudolph Ackermann, P. and D. Colnaghi, Henry Graves, Thomas Agnew, Thomas McLean, and the Frenchmen, Ernest Gambart and Louis Victor Flatow.

The publishers acted as middlemen between the painter and the public and sometimes commissioned artists to paint subjects specifically for reproduction. Since painting and copyright were separate saleable commodities, the publisher usually attempted to buy both. Very high prices were paid to painters. Thomas Agnew paid William Hunt £10,500 for *The Shadow of Death* in 1874, possibly the highest price ever paid for painting and engraving rights until that time. Proceeds from the sale of proofs alone netted the publisher over £20,000, and the engravings were in continual demand for the next fifty years.[20] Returns to the publishers were therefore enormous. Once both painting and copyright were in their possession they could sell admissions to view the painting, and by exhibiting and promoting the painting they could sell subscriptions for the print. Their exhibitions of new paintings by popular artists sometimes gathered larger crowds than contemporary shows at the Royal Academy.

Print dealers were accused by engraver John Burnet of keeping certain painters "constantly before the public, to the exclusion of all others, hence it is that several artists have had the whole command of the market."[21] The accusation that the publishers were the dictators of the art market is probably quite justified. As Jeremy Maas has noted,

> it was the printsellers who were the unacknowledged legislators of the art world. It was they who carried an artist's reputation into every home in the country and to all four corners of the globe; it was they who brought prosperity to the artists and, of course, to themselves.... It was no mere chance that these leviathans of the art trade were called princes. The foremost of them made large fortunes, and lived on a princely scale.[22]

The large amounts of money to be made selling prints also resulted in large-scale corruption, which caused print dealers to band together in 1847 to form the Printsellers' Association. With a membership consisting of all the influential print publishers in London, along with representatives from provincial centres, the association hoped to regulate and control the publication of prints. Its purpose was to remedy the corruption that had arisen with the advent of steel plates and the subsequent proliferation of "proofs." Proofs in the past had been limited to the small number of impressions pulled from a copper plate before the engraving was completed and the lettering added. Because of their rarity, and the crispness of the impressions, they traditionally demanded higher prices. However, hundreds, perhaps thousands of "proofs" were pulled from single steel plates by unscrupulous publishers. In 1847 the Printsellers' Association, in an attempt to control the situation, required all publishers to list with them the number of proofs taken and their prices; the association's distinctive stamp was then added to each impression.

Even with these regulations, the numbers and kinds of proofs are baffling. Artist's Proofs were seen as the most desirable and were stamped in the margin in the lower left corner. Presentation Proofs, Before Letters Proofs, Lettered Proofs, and all other classes of proofs were stamped in the lower right.[23] The stamp seen on a number of works in the exhibition indicates that they are artist's proofs. Most of this group are also signed in pencil by both the painter and the engraver, demonstrating the approval of the painter and his endorsement of the work of the engraver.

The Art Union of London

Although London dealers had widespread and almost dictatorial control over the art market, another independent organization attempted to aid the cause of contemporary art: the Art Union of London, founded in 1836. The avowed aim of the Art Union was "to cultivate and extend the love of the Arts of Painting and Sculpture and to give encouragement to Artists."[24] The Art Union held annual free exhibitions and published a series of volumes called *The Art Union Prize Annual,* which were illustrated with small engravings. Essentially, the organization was an art lottery. Subscribers paid a guinea or more annually for the opportunity to win a painting of their choice, to be selected from current London exhibitions, and all subscribers received an engraving annually, usually after one of the prize paintings. This practice could be applauded when the winning subscriber chose an example such as *The Journey to Emmaus,* painted and engraved by John Linnell (No. 48), but often the works were much more insignificant and the Art Union was criticized for belittling the cause of art rather than encouraging it.

In the 1840s William Makepeace Thackery wrote in scathing language of the "Tart-Union," whose practices would do nothing other than "degrade Art."[25] Thackery maintained that the organization encouraged artists to paint to suit public taste, and since the public was ignorant and had bad taste, he concluded that both the public and the painter were degraded. He claimed that artists no longer painted for the sake of art but for the sake of the Art Union.[26]

The Art Union of London and small provincial lotteries and unions continued, nevertheless, to flourish financially, despite a move to suppress them in 1844. In 1847 the Art Union achieved a peak in subscriptions of £17,871.[27] Its success in reaching a wide audience is documented in the annual report of 1860:

> [The Art Union] sent some hundreds of engravings over the world, - to the gold-diggers of Australia, the backwoodsmen of Canada, to New Zealand, China, the Indies, Egypt, the United States; in fact, to nearly every corner of the globe where there is an English settlement, as well as to every city, town, and village of the United Kingdom.[28]

Among their publications was the *The Road to Ruin* series after William Powell Frith (1819-1909), released in 1878 and again in 1882 (nos. 63-67).

Other Subjects and Techniques

With the paintings *Derby Day* and *The Railway Station* and the subsequent engravings, Frith had become the painter of the new urban subject. *The Road to Ruin* was one of two series he painted with Hogarth in mind. This group of five paintings was etched by the Belgian printmaker Leopold Flameng (1831-1911) and chronicles the downfall of a young writer who allows alcohol and gambling to control him until he loses everything he cherishes and is finally driven to take his own life. Even by the 1880s when the prints were published, the obvious moralizing that dominated the earlier Victorian period still had a large audience.

The etching technique employed in this series firmly dates it to the 1870s, when etching became a viable alternative to mixed methods. It was inevitable that the public would eventually seek novel techniques, and in 1876, P.G. Hammerton wrote that "Etching from pictures has in fact become a regular business and many artists have taken to it as a resource when painting or engraving with the burin did not bring sufficient income."[29]

The Paris Commune of 1870 led to an influx of exiled French artists, including a number of important etchers, some of whom began to reproduce popular English paintings. Emile Boilvin (1845-1899), who etched several important plates after Sir Edward Burne-Jones (1833-1898), and James Tissot (1836-1902) (No. 68) were among the more noteworthy immigrants.

Coinciding with the developing fashion for etching was the revival of the pure mezzotint technique and a proliferation of photo-mechanical processes, all of which were linked to new varieties of subject matter. As anecdotal subjects became *passé* by the end of the century, Victorian art entered its neo-classical phase with painters such as Sir Albert Moore (1841-1893), Lord Frederick Leighton (1830-1896), and Sir Edward Poynter (1836-1919). Reproductions of the works of these painters were most often made using etching or pure mezzotint for small editions and photogravure for larger runs.

By the 1860s, another important technical innovation, "steel facing," had been perfected, through which etched or engraved copper plates were coated with a thin film of steel through galvanic action. Engravers and etchers could again work on the more desirable, softer metal while retaining the durability of steel. At the first signs of wear the steel could be removed and the plate re-faced to prolong the life of the plate indefinitely. By the last quarter of the century most etchings, pure mezzotints, and photogravures were made on copper plates.

The revival of pure as opposed to mixed mezzotint coincided with a revival of interest in several eighteenth-century painters including Sir Joshua Reynolds and Thomas Gainsborough, whose paintings fetched large sums between 1870 and 1920. Mezzotints after their works were again in demand, and Samuel Cousins achieved the most acclaim for portrait mezzotints after Reynolds.[30] The reproduction of contemporary paintings, including Albert Moore's *Dreamers* engraved by Thomas Gooch Appleton (1854-1924) (No. 69), also was affected by this return to pure mezzotint. This technique, along with the practice of printing in brown and the trend toward smaller editions, reflect the current fashion for rarity and novelty, as opposed to the homogeneous techniques and large quantities demanded of the mixed-method engravings. Also catering to a smaller, more elite audience was Sir Frank Short (1857-c.1906), who executed several fine mezzotints after George Frederick Watts (1817-1904) during this period.

The photogravure technique, which combined photography with engraving, appealed to a widening audience because it provided more exact copies of original paintings. According to Sir Hubert Herkomer writing in 1892, "the severe imitation of 'paint-manner' is a thing of our time" and the success of photography was inevitable when mixed methods were characterized by "proneness to exaggerated care in the imitation of the surface of a picture."[31] By closely imitating "paint-manner," the mixed-method engraving became so photographic in appearance that it was easily replaced by photography, which promised larger editions and lower costs. Finally, photomechanical methods rendered the reproductive print obsolete.

Certainly other factors dealt the death blow. With the market flooded by large engravings of popular contemporary paintings, it was natural that public taste should eventually be sated. Original printmaking, especially etching, could then step in. Spokesmen like Sir Seymour Haden made careful distinctions between painter-etchers and professional engravers, and attempted to convince the public that small, spontaneously etched original compositions were preferable to large, "mechanically" reproduced engravings.

In a lecture given in America in 1883, Haden "confronted the engravers with the reflection that their 'trade' was not endangered, as etching was for the cultured few, and the *hoi polloi* would always prefer to buy 'good, big, handsome' engravings."[32] Haden would have been very pleased to know that within thirty-five years not even the general public would be clamouring for "big, handsome" engravings. The desire for originality in the twentieth century meant that by the 1920s many reproductive prints were on the way to the pulp mills. Their disrepute has continued until the present day.

The progression of the reproductive print toward ultimate redundancy began in the late eighteenth century, when several new techniques were adopted to reproduce drawings and paintings more accurately. These inventions were created in response to a demand from the small but expanding print audience. As the print public grew at an enormous rate from the early to mid-nineteenth century, so did the disregard for the engraver's independent ability to interpret and the desire for more "photographic" copies. Thus, at the same time that Victorian ideals and tastes were being disseminated around the world through engravings, production for the masses was resulting in a decline in artistic input and quality.[33] In 1911 Arthur Hind lamented that the "general public calls for reproductions of pictures, and does not stop to think... of the value of interpretation in the hands of a real artist-engraver. What it demands is the fidelity of the photographer, not a print which is in itself a real work of art."[34] His comment concisely sums up the ultimate fate of the reproductive print.

GEORGE BAXTER'S OIL-COLOUR PRINTS

45. GEORGE BAXTER (British, 1804-1867)
after an unknown painter

News from Australia 1854
Oil-colour print using one aquatint steel plate and twelve colour wood blocks on wove paper
11.1 x 15.0 cm (sheet)
Bequest of Mr. John G. Lee
Acc. no. 55/15

C.T. Courtney Lewis, Baxter's biographer, lists *News from Australia* as one of "The Best Prints for the Decoration of Homes." He adds that "for smaller places and well within sight we like 'News from Home' and 'News from Australia.'"[35] The two companion oil-colour prints recorded the recent emigration of British subjects to Australia in search of gold, and the happy reception of news by relatives or friends on opposite sides of the globe. Such works could also be pasted into pocketbooks, scrapbooks, and needle cases, making them truly popular art.

Baxter devised his process to imitate oil painting or watercolour by using an initial key intaglio plate or lithographic stone in a neutral colour, with ten to as many as thirty colour wood blocks. The refinement of a registration system and the careful selection and integration of colours demonstrate Baxter's consistent concern with craftsmanship. His lack of business sense and the expense of his elaborate printing process, however, led to endless financial difficulties. After 1849 he was forced to sell licenses to other printmakers, many of whom were more concerned with high production at low costs than with quality.

NINETEENTH-CENTURY WOOD ENGRAVING

46. DALZIEL BROTHERS
after WILLIAM HOLMAN HUNT (British, 1827-1910)

Go and Come, in *Good Words,* 1862, p. 32
Wood engraving
14.0 x 10.3 cm (image)
The Alan Garrow Collection in the E.P. Taylor Reference Library, Art Gallery of Ontario

47. DALZIEL BROTHERS
after JOHN EVERETT MILLAIS (British, 1829-1896)

The Lost Piece of Silver from *The Parables of Our Lord and Saviour Jesus Christ* in *Good Words,* 1863, facing p. 605
Wood engraving
13.8 x 10.8 cm (image)
The Alan Garrow Collection in the E.P. Taylor Reference Library, Art Gallery of Ontario

Good Words, founded in 1860, was a "popular, semi-religious sixpenny magazine," one of several periodicals illustrated with wood engravings that enjoyed wide circulation in the 1850s and 1860s.[36] In 1862 *Good Words* added William Holman Hunt to its list of illustrators. Hunt's predisposition toward symbolic Biblical subjects was an asset in illustrating poems such as *Go and Come.* The inscription below the image reads "The Sun is high in heaven, the harvest but begun." The work was engraved by the most famous firm of nineteenth-century wood-engravers, the Dalziel brothers.

John Everett Millais drew *The Lost Piece of Silver* for a series called *The Parables of Our Lord,* which were engraved and published in proof editions by the Dalziels in 1862 and 1863. Twelve of the parables also appeared throughout 1863 in *Good Words* as illustrations for a series of articles by Reverend Thomas Guthrie called "The Parables in Light of the Present Day." The impressions in *Good Words* (No. 47) were pulled from electrotypes, metal copies of the original wood blocks, because the Dalziels wanted to preserve the blocks for the book published in 1864.

Millais was apparently delighted with the challenge of the project and with the results when printed. He drew the pen-and-ink designs directly onto the wood blocks; they were thereby destroyed in the engraving process. In *The Lost Piece of Silver,* closely laid lines are used to build up the textures of the garment and the face of the searching woman, who is illuminated by the soft light of the candle and the mysterious light of the moon. *The Lost Piece of Silver* was one of two parables that Millais used as the basis for an oil painting. The painting was exhibited at the Royal Academy in 1862 but was later destroyed in a gas explosion.[37]

THE POPULARITY OF BIBLICAL IMAGERY

48. JOHN LINNELL (British, 1792-1882)
after his own painting

The Journey to Emmaus 1839
Mezzotint and etching on india paper
37.8 x 48.0 cm (imp.)
Gift of F.M. Kimbark
Acc. no. 81/528

John Linnell's long career extends from the early nineteenth century to almost the end of the Victorian period. He is perhaps best remembered for his patronage of Wil-

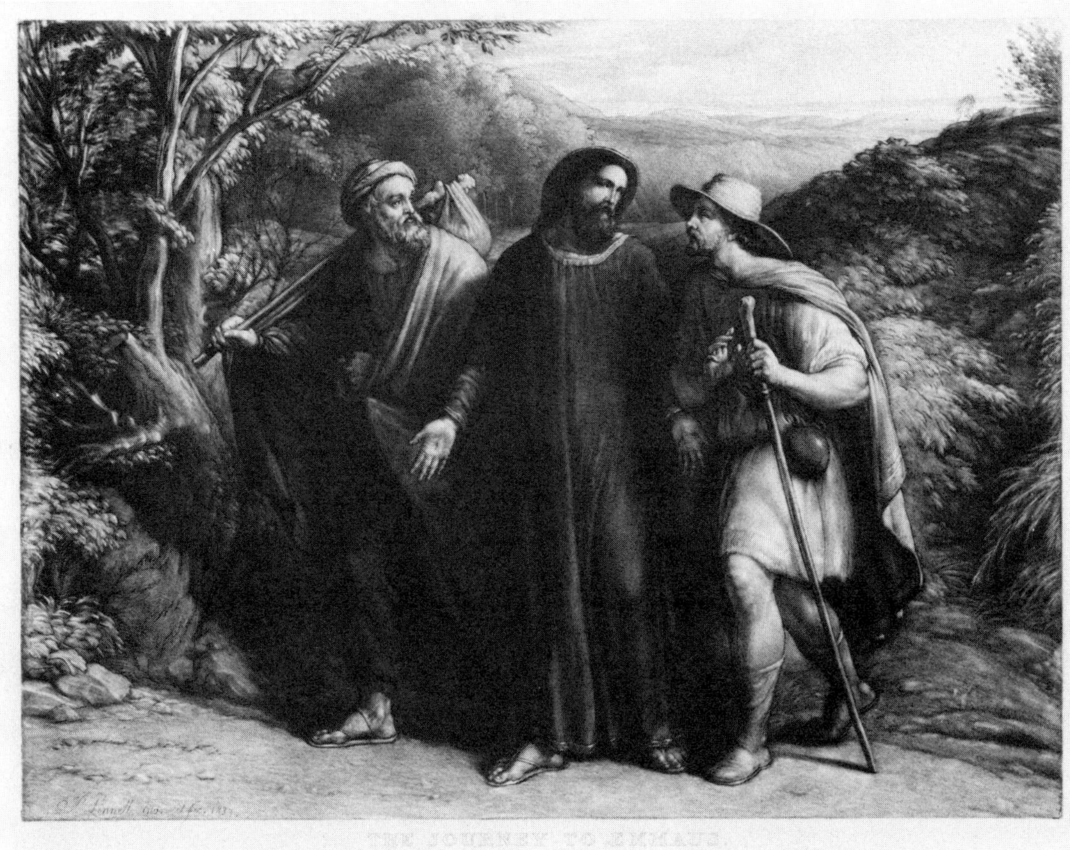

48. Linnell, *The Journey to Emmaus,* 1839

liam Blake (1757-1827) and for his association with the group of artists that idolized Blake, "The Ancients" at Shoreham. He was primarily a landscapist and a portraitist but occasionally painted religious subjects, reproducing many of the images in mezzotint and etching.

Although Linnell produced a few plates around 1818 that may have been influenced by Blake's style, he also developed techniques that would appeal to wider audiences. In *The Journey to Emmaus* he has combined two processes, mezzotint for tonal areas and etching for defining forms. This combination was often used for reproductive prints during the first half of the century (see nos. 4, 34 and 35). *The Journey to Emmaus* describes Christ's appearance to two disciples after his Resurrection (Luke 24). Linnell exhibited the painting at the Royal Academy in 1835 and it is now in the Ashmolean Museum, Oxford. In 1838 Linnell was commissioned by the Art Union of London to engrave a reproduction which was distributed to subscribers the following year.

49. LUMB STOCKS (British, 1812-1892)
after JAMES ECKFORD LAUDER (British, 1811-1869)

The Wise and Foolish Virgins 1846
Line-engraving and etching on wove paper
46.0 x 66.0 cm (imp.)
Gift of F.M. Kimbark
Acc. no. 81/534

James Eckford Lauder's painting, *The Ten Virgins,* was exhibited at the Royal Academy in 1844. Two years later the Association for the Promotion of the Fine Arts in Scotland published the line-engraving by Lumb Stocks. The subject is taken from Matthew 25 and describes five dishevelled, foolish virgins who are not prepared for the arrival of the bridegroom, and five immaculately dressed, wise virgins who wait in anticipation of his coming. The lamps of the wise illuminate the scene, casting their foolish sisters into shadow and suggesting the ultimate plight of the latter: rejection from the marriage feast and eternal damnation.

MIXED-METHOD ENGRAVING AND ANECDOTAL SUBJECTS

FREDERICK HOLLYER (British, fl. 1860s)
after EDWIN LANDSEER (British, 1802-1873)

50. *The Old Shepherd's Chief Mourner* 1869 A.P.
Mixed mezzotint on india paper
65.6 x 71.0 cm (imp.)
Purchase, 1982
Acc. no. 82/137
Printsellers' Association Stamp: OTI

51. *The Shepherd's Grave* 1868
Mixed mezzotint on wove paper
65.5 x 71.0 cm (imp.)
Purchase, 1982
Acc. no. 82/138

Landseer's painting, *The Shepherd's Grave,* was first exhibited in 1829 at the British Institution as *The Poor Dog.* It was the forerunner to *The Old Shepherd's Chief Mourner,* which was shown at the Royal Academy in 1837 and which became the most famous among Landseer's paintings of similar subjects.[38] John Ruskin was entranced by *The Old Shepherd's Chief Mourner,* calling it "one of the most perfect poems or pictures... modern times have seen."[39] The painting was engraved initially in 1838 by B.P. Gibbon and is a classic mid-Victorian image, combining anecdote and realistic detail to create a sentimental, poignant picture. Only one hundred artist's proofs of Hollyer's engraving were issued by J. McQueen in 1869.

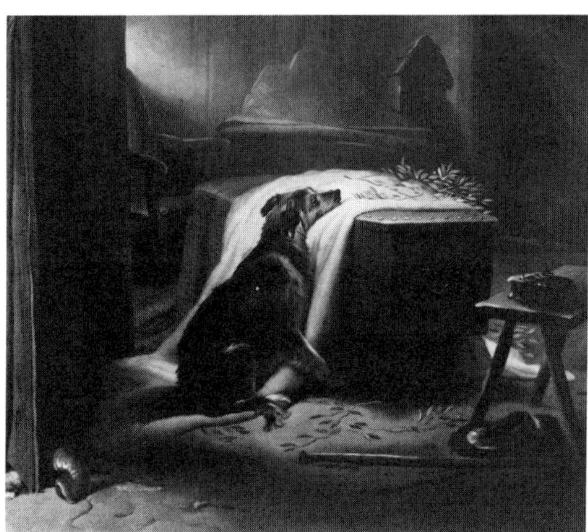

50. Hollyer after Landseer, *The Old Shepherd's Chief Mourner,* 1869

52. WILLIAM HENRY SIMMONS (British, 1811-1882)
after THOMAS BROOKS (British, 1818-1891)

Contrition 1859
Mixed mezzotint on wove paper
70.5 x 56.8 cm (imp.)
Gift of F.M. Kimbark
Acc. no. 81/532

Thomas Brooks exhibited *Contrition* at the 1858 Royal Academy with the quotation, "The Lord is nigh into them that are of a broken heart." The following year Henry Graves published the engraving by W.H. Simmons. Simmons was one of the most talented engravers that the Victorian period produced. His mixed mezzotint technique helps to convey the heavy melancholic mood of the narrative.

Although the meaning of *Contrition* is ambiguous, the man of the house seems to be at the point of decision; he must decide whether to return to his life of drunkenness and gambling as symbolized by the objects in the room behind, or repent in the manner of his tiny daughter. Other symbols, for example, the Bible in the brightly lit foreground, probably have a two-fold function, representing solace for the unfortunate woman and conviction for her wayward husband.

Henry Graves and Company was one of the most influential publishing firms of the period, and a member of the Printsellers' Association from 1847 to 1894, issuing over a thousand plates (Nos. 53 and 69 were also published by Graves).

53. SAMUEL COUSINS (British, 1801-1887)
after THOMAS FAED (British, 1826-1900)

The Mitherless Bairn 1860 W. 191 A.P.
Mixed mezzotint on india paper
68.0 x 87.5 cm (imp.)
Signed in pencil lower right: Samuel Cousins;
lower left: "Thomas Faed"
Bequest of John Ross Robertson, 1947
Acc. no. 47/23
Printsellers' Association stamp: LUV

The painting *The Mitherless Bairn* is currently in the collection of The National Gallery of Victoria, Melbourne, Australia. It was painted and originally exhibited by Faed at the Royal Academy in 1855 with two verses from a poem of the same name by a contemporary Scottish poet, William Thom. The poem describes the plight of an orphan whose mother died at his birth. Cousins' engraving of the subject was exhibited at the Royal Academy six years later in 1861. The impression exhibited then was probably one of 475 artist's proofs.

Like Landseer's *The Old Shepherd's Chief Mourner, The*

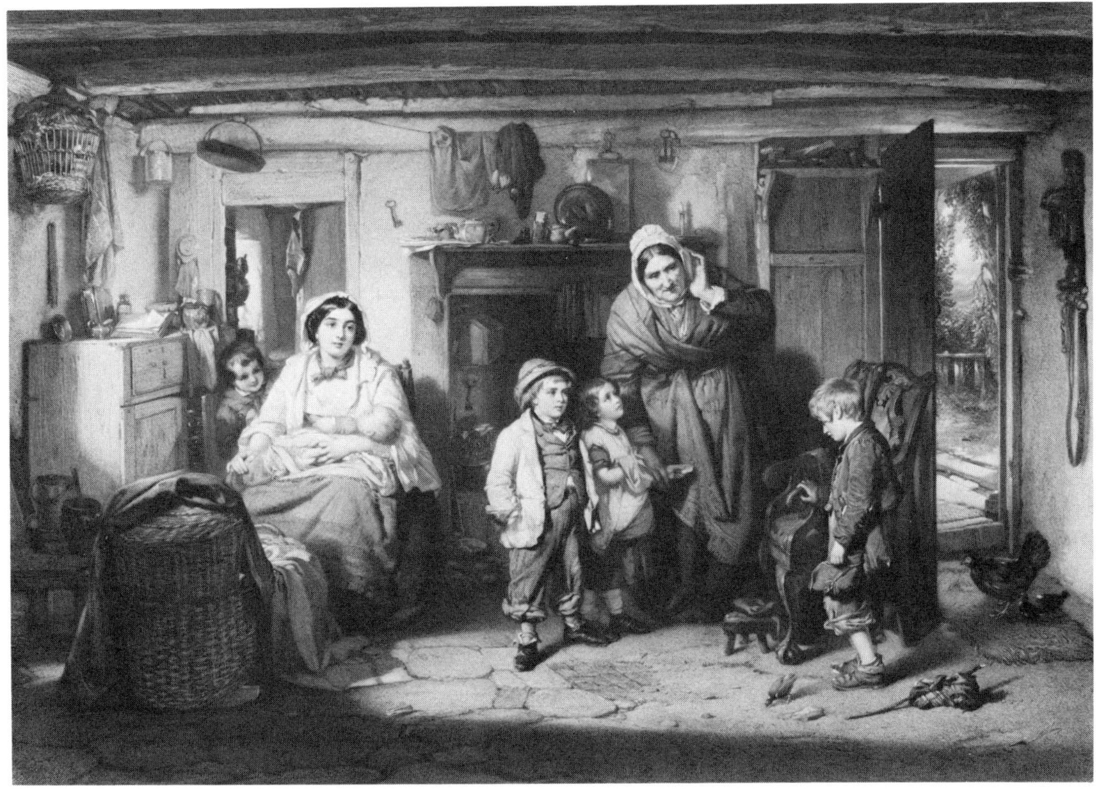

53. Cousins after Faed, *The Mitherless Bairn,* 1860

Mitherless Bairn was Faed's first great popular success, leading to his continued production of rustic, Highland scenes. Faed recognized the value of the print both for the sale of the copyright and for advertisement for his painting. He negotiated shrewdly with his publisher, Henry Graves, for his own terms and for the engraver of his choice.[40]

Samuel Cousins learned the fundamentals of mezzotint engraving from S.W. Reynolds, who was also David Lucas' teacher (see nos. 39 and 40). Gaining prestige through mezzotints after Thomas Lawrence and Joshua Reynolds, Cousins became the best known Victorian engraver, and the first to be elected as a full Academician of the Royal Academy in 1855.

54. FREDERICK STACPOOLE (British, 1813-1907)
after THOMAS FAED (British, 1826-1900)

Worn Out 1871 A.P.
Mixed mezzotint on india paper
58.5 x 71.2 cm (imp.)
Signed in pencil lower right: F. Stacpoole; lower left: Thomas Faed
Bequest of John Ross Robertson, 1947
Acc. no. 47/30
Printsellers' Association Stamp: HPH

Worn Out, another in Faed's series of rustic interiors, was exhibited at the Royal Academy in 1868. Stacpoole exhibited his engraving of the painting three years later. Originally trained as a portrait painter, Stacpoole returned to oil painting as he grew older. Most of his career, however, was devoted to reproducing paintings in the mixed mezzotint technique.

The print publishers Pilegram and Lefèvre issued only two hundred artist's proofs of Stacpoole's *Worn Out.* Ernest Gambart began the Pilegram and Lefèvre firm earlier in the century as Gambart and Company, and he became one of the richest and most successful publishers of the Victorian period.

WILLIAM HENRY SIMMONS (British, 1811-1882)
after ERSKINE NICOL (British, 1825-1904)

55. *Steady, Johnnie, Steady* 1874 A.P.
Mixed method on india paper
76.0 x 60.0 cm (imp.)
Signed in pencil lower left: Erskine Nicol, lower right: W.H. Simmons
Bequest of John Ross Robertson, 1947
Acc. no. 47/31
Printsellers' Association Stamp: DBC

56. *Looking Out for a Safe Investment* 1878 A.P.
Mixed method on india paper
76.0 x 59.0 cm (imp.)
Signed in pencil lower left: Erskine Nicol; lower right: W.H. Simmons
Bequest of John Ross Robertson, 1947
Acc. no. 47/33
Printsellers' Association stamp: VSP

Another painter known for his Scottish Highland themes, Erskine Nicol exhibited *Steady, Johnnie, Steady* at the Royal Academy in 1873 and *Looking Out for a Safe Investment* in 1876. The publication dates for the engravings of 1874 and 1877 respectively, illustrate the speed with which an accomplished engraver could complete a plate using the mixed method. Simmons exhibited *Steady, Johnnie, Steady* at the Royal Academy in 1875. The Printsellers' Association lists 275 artist's proofs for *Looking Out for a Safe Investment* and 200 for the earlier plate. The two engravings were published simultaneously in London and in New York, emphasizing that by the Victorian period the audience for English prints had extended beyond the continent and had become world-wide. Anecdotal subjects of children were crowd-pleasers everywhere.

Simmons received early training from the line-engraver William Finden (1787-1852). His engravings after Nicol combine etching, line-engraving, and stipple on an aquatint base, rather than the standard mezzotint foundation.

57. FRANCIS HOLL (British, 1815-1885)
after GEORGE ELGAR HICKS (British, 1824-1914)

Il Penseroso 1868 A.P.
Line-engraving and etching on india paper
74.0 x 42.7 cm (imp.)
Gift of F.M. Kimbark
Acc. no. 81/526
Printsellers' Association stamp: EEA

George Elgar Hicks exhibited the painting at the Royal

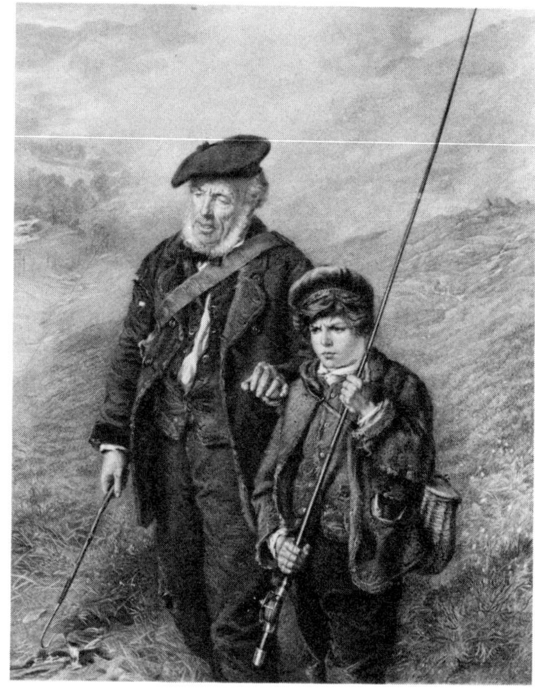

55. Simmons after Nicol, *Steady, Johnnie, Steady,* 1874

Academy in 1865 with the quotation, "There let the pealing organ blow... And bring all heaven before mine eyes," from John Milton's poem *Il Penseroso*. Its companion, *L'Allegro*, portrays a happy, active young woman who acts as a foil to the thoughtful, quiet mood of the goddess of contemplation. The figures are contained within Gothic arches, which add to the aura of religiosity and meditation. They were engraved by Holl and published as pendants in 1868 with 300 artist's proofs each, and were sold both singly and in pairs.

Francis Holl came from a family of engravers and learned the craft from his father, the stipple engraver William Holl (1771-1838). Francis usually combined line-engraving and stipple and *Il Penseroso* is executed primarily in line augmented with stipple.

SAMUEL COUSINS (British, 1801-1887)
after JOHN EVERETT MILLAIS (British, 1829-1896)

58. *Yes or No?* 1873 W.222 A.P.
Mixed mezzotint on india paper
60.5 x 46.7 cm (imp.)
Signed in pencil lower right: Samuel Cousins; lower left: John Everett Millais
Bequest of John Ross Robertson, 1947
Acc. no. 47/24
Printsellers' Association stamp: EFA

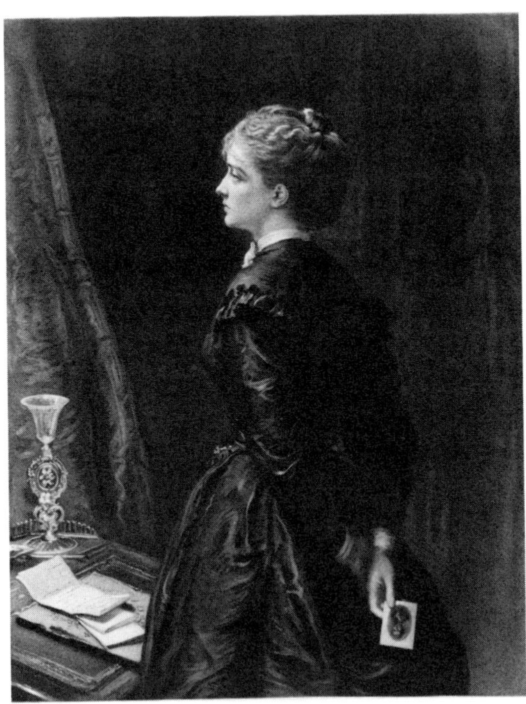

58. Cousins after Millais, *Yes or No?*, 1873

59. *No!* 1876 W.223 A.P.
Mixed mezzotint on india paper
61.0 x 43.5 cm (imp.)
Signed in pencil lower right: Samuel Cousins, lower left: J. Everett Millais
Bequest of John Ross Robertson, 1947
Acc. no. 47/25
Printsellers' Association stamp: OAZ

60. *Yes!* 1878 W. 224 A.P.
Mixed mezzotint on india paper
69.8 x 55.7 cm (imp.)
Signed in pencil lower right: Samuel Cousins; lower left: John Everett Millais
Bequest of John Ross Robertson, 1947
Acc. no. 47/26
Printsellers' Association stamp: FQQ

Millais' canvases for this series were exhibited at the Royal Academy in 1871, 1875 and 1877, respectively. Thomas Agnew published Cousin's engravings with 375 artist's proofs of *Yes or No?* and 500 each of *No!* and *Yes!*

The proliferation of paintings of courtship subjects by the 1870s testifies to the central importance of marriage in Victorian society. Images of the proposal were particular favorites.[41] In Millais' first painting the young woman, with the photograph of her suitor in one hand and his written proposal on the table before her, faces the difficult question, "Yes or No?" In the second image she ponders over the resolute "No" that she has just penned. Although Millais apparently found this to be a satisfactory ending, subsequent public lobbying forced him to finish the story with *Yes!*[42]

The publisher, Thomas Agnew, probably began to sell the engravings in sets as soon as the third was issued, as a 1905 catalogue suggests.[43] Curiously, the catalogue illustrates *No!* on the left, *Yes or No?* on the right, and *Yes!* in the centre. This arrangement may make sense in terms of compositional balance, but it also creates a very jumbled reading of the story.

A comparison between Cousins' *Yes or No?* and Millais' *Yes or No?* (Yale University Art Gallery) illustrates the general fact that engravings were often more detailed than their models. Cousins has filled in the spatially ambiguous background with textured drapery and a deeper recession in space. Objects such as the glass vase, the letter, and the photograph are clearly defined. The script on the letter is almost legible and the totally obscured face on the *carte de visite* in the painting is nearly recognizable as the suitor who finally arrives in *Yes!* Details of dress and hair are also brought into sharper focus and the heroine looks calmer, nobler and less distraught than in the painting. The comparison suggests that although engravers usually attempted to copy faithfully, the limitations of their techniques or their own inventiveness led them to "add" to the original image, and sometimes to idealize their models.

By the 1870s Cousins was a very distinguished engraver and could demand his own terms. When the prestigious publishers Thomas Agnew approached him in 1873 to engrave *Yes or No?*, he required half the fee (600 guineas) when the plate was half finished and the balance upon completion.[44]

61. SAMUEL COUSINS (British, 1801-1887)
after JOHN EVERETT MILLAIS (British, 1829-1896)

The Princes in the Tower 1879 W.221 A.P.
Mixed mezzotint on india paper
77.5 x 50.5 cm (imp.)
Signed in pencil lower right: Samuel Cousins; lower left: John Everett Millais
Bequest of John Ross Robertson, 1947
Acc. no. 47/22
Printsellers' Association Stamp: T.U.K.

Millais' painting is now in the Royal Holloway College, University of London. It was first exhibited at the Royal Academy in 1878. A year later Cousins' engraving in the mixed mezzotint technique was also shown at a Royal

Academy exhibition. The engraving was published by the Fine Art Society in 1879 with 600 artist's proofs.

The Princes in the Tower was considered by Millais to be a companion to his *Princess Elizabeth in St. James*.[45] Millais' concern in both was to recreate accurately the historic dress and location and to convey the terror of the young victims. The *Princes in the Tower* captures the moment before Prince Edward V and his brother Richard were murdered by assassins working for their uncle, Richard of Gloucester. The subject had been a favourite with artists for almost one hundred years.[46] Cousins' detailed rendering faithfully conveys the overall mood of the original painting. In black and white the image is perhaps more somber and the darkness more ominous.

62. HUBERT HERKOMER (British, 1849-1914)
after JOHN EVERETT MILLAIS (British, 1829-1896)

Caller Herrin' 1882 *Remarque* Proof
Mixed mezzotint on india paper
68.5 x 53.0 cm
Signed in pencil lower left: J.E. Millais, lower right: Hubert Herkomer
Bequest of John Ross Robertson, 1947
Acc. no. 47/27
Printsellers' Association stamp: XDP

John Everett Millais' painting *Caller Herrin'* portrays a young fishseller who has temporarily forgotten the drudgery of her everyday existence and is lost in faraway thought.[47] It was exhibited by the Fine Art Society in their London gallery in 1882, and engraved by Hubert Herkomer the same year.

This impression is one of only fifty *remarque* proofs. The *remarques,* found in the lower margin, are portraits of the painter on the left and the engraver on the right. Although *remarques* were not uncommon in English prints at this time, they were rarely found in reproductive engravings. The portraits, and their accompanying pencil signatures, are a charming addition to the engraving, and speak of the close partnership between the two artists.

Reproductive engraving was only one of the many careers of Hubert Herkomer. He was also a painter, writer, founder of an art school, opera composer, actor, and stage designer, and was knighted in 1907. In his book, *Etching and Mezzotint Engraving,* written in 1892, he discussed the value of the reproductive print, advocating etching or pure mezzotint as the best techniques to interpret painting. Many of his earlier works, including *Caller Herrin,* had been in the mixed method, but he expressed regret for having used it because he had come to feel that it imitated "paint-manner" without interpreting the painter's underlying intent.[48]

ALTERNATIVES TO THE MIXED METHOD

LEOPOLD FLAMENG (Belgian, 1831-1911)
after WILLIAM POWELL FRITH (British, 1819-1909)

63. *The Road to Ruin: I College* 1882
Etching on wove paper
44.0 x 53.0 cm (imp.)
Gift of F.M. Kimbark
Acc. no. 81/524.1

64. *The Road to Ruin: II Ascot* 1882
Etching on wove paper
44.0 x 53.0 cm (imp.)
Gift of F.M. Kimbark
Acc. no. 81/524.2

65. *The Road to Ruin: III Arrest* 1882
Etching on wove paper
44.3 x 53.0 cm (imp.)
Gift of F.M. Kimbark
Acc. no. 81/524.3

66. *The Road to Ruin: IV Struggles* 1882
Etching on wove paper
44.3 x 53.0 cm (imp.)
Gift of F.M. Kimbark
Acc. no. 81/524.4

67. *The Road to Ruin: V The End* 1882
Etching on wove paper
44.5 x 53.0 cm (imp.)
Gift of F.M. Kimbark
Acc. no. 81/524.5

W.P. Frith exhibited his series of five paintings *The Road to Ruin* at the Royal Academy in 1878.[49] He noted in his memoirs that "the copyright was purchased by the Art Union of London, and the pictures were etched by one of the greatest professors of that art in France."[50] The printmaker was Leopold Flameng, who etched many plates after both French and English painters.

Etching had been revived in the nineteenth century by a group of original printmakers, but it also provided an alternative for reproductive prints when the public began to tire of mixed-method engravings. The Art Union published *The Road to Ruin* in 1878 and again in 1882. The complete set of five etchings is apparently quite rare.[51]

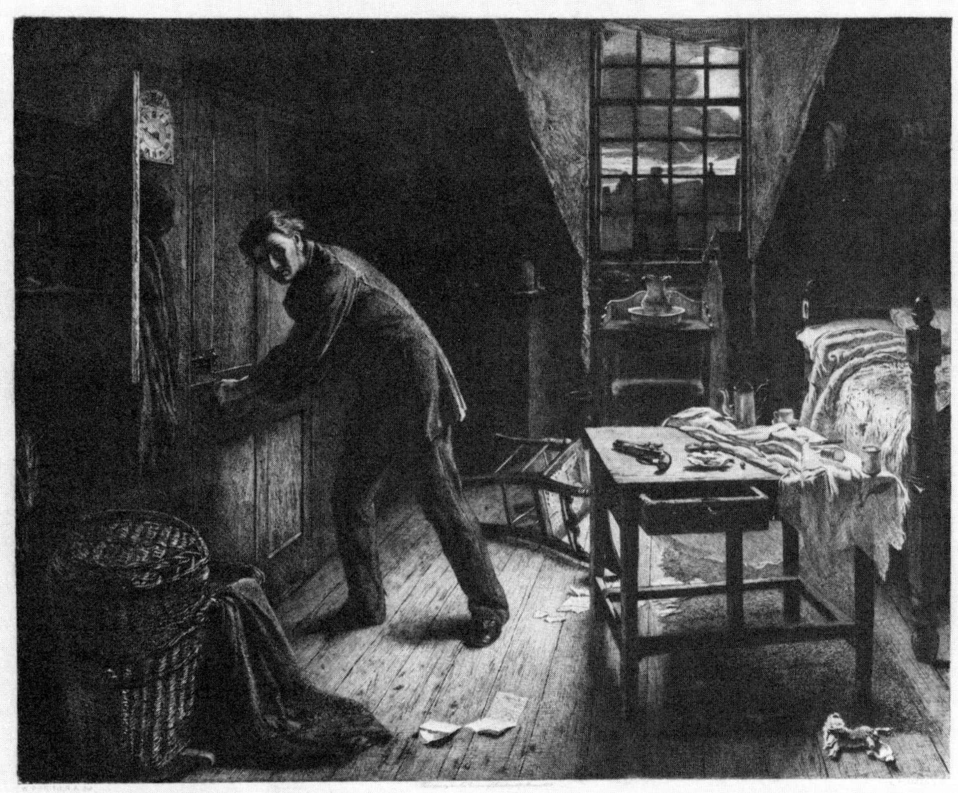

67. Flameng after Frith, *The End*, 1882

The series was recognized in the nineteenth century as the Victorian version of Hogarth's *The Rake's Progress*, even though the painter contended that

> without any pretension to do my work on Hogarthian lines, I thought I could show some of the evils of gambling; my idea being a kind of gambler's progress, avoiding the satirical view of Hogarth, for which I knew myself to be unfitted. I desired to trace the career of the youth from his college days to his ruin and death – a victim of one of the most fatal vices.[52]

68. JAMES TISSOT (French, 1836-1902)
after his own painting

Sans Dot 1885 W.79
Etching and drypoint on laid paper
39.9 x 25.2 cm (imp.)
Purchase, 1972
Acc. no. 71/375

Tissot began his *La Femme à Paris* series in 1883 and completed the fifteen paintings in 1885. Each canvas describes a Parisian woman in a different social situation. Public response was not enthusiastic because the works were caught "between the conventions of Victorian narrative painting and the avant-garde [and therefore] they pleased hardly anyone."[53] In *Sans Dot* Tissot reflects on the plight of a young female without a dowry, who is physically separated from the handsome soldiers and happy crowd of people behind by empty space and by a barrier of chairs, and has only an old woman as a companion.[54] The radical cropping of the image that was derived from photography or Japanese prints, the staring faces seen through the trees, and the frozen glance and pose of the Parisian woman give the work a modern quality of psychological unease.

Tissot escaped from the French Commune in 1871 and fled to England, where he spent eleven years developing his etching technique and receiving acclaim for his paintings of modern urban subjects. He was very aware of the commercial possibilities of reproductive prints and approximately half his etchings and mezzotints were interpretations of works in other media, usually painting.

Upon completion of the *La Femme à Paris* paintings, he planned to issue etchings in three sets of five with 500 impressions each. Only the first five were completed and the editions seem to have been smaller than originally planned, perhaps less than 100 impressions from each plate.[55]

69. THOMAS GOOCH APPLETON (British, 1854-1924)
after ALBERT JOSEPH MOORE (British, 1841-1893)

Dreamers 1898 A.P.
Mezzotint in brown ink on india paper
54.7 x 78.0 cm (imp.)
Signed in pencil lower right: Thomas G. Appleton
Gift of F.M. Kimbark
Acc. no. 81/519
Printsellers' Association Stamp: TVJ

Albert Moore's *Dreamers* was exhibited in the Royal Academy in 1882 and is now in the Birmingham City Museum and Art Gallery in Birmingham, England. It was engraved in mezzotint by T.G. Appleton, a well known portrait engraver, and published in 1898 by Henry Graves. The plate was destroyed after only 525 proofs were printed, 250 of which were artist's proofs. While most Victorian engravings were published with a limited edition of proofs, almost unlimited numbers of ordinary prints, which were not declared to the Printsellers' Association were subsequently pulled from the plate. The practice of limiting editions by destroying the plates became increasingly fashionable toward the end of the century, when rarity was particularly valued. Similarly, the return to pure mezzotint and the use of brown ink were signs of the search for novelty as well as of an admiration for eighteenth-century techniques.

Albert Moore was a High Victorian painter who sought to remove all expressive emotion from his skilfully constructed, essentially subjectless paintings. In *Dreamers*, the draped bodies of three statuesque females are carefully balanced against a busy, decorative background. The rich folds of the drapery and the patterning translate well into mezzotint.

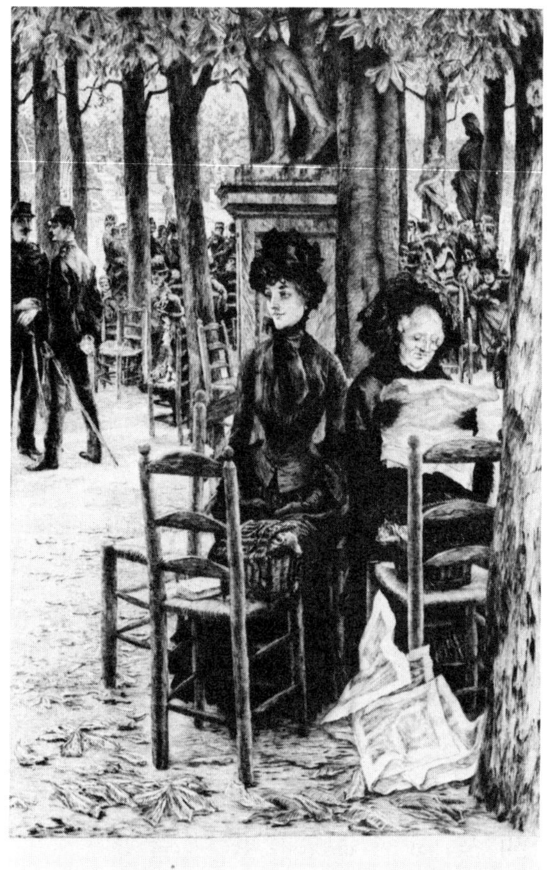

68. Tissot, *Sans Dot,* 1885

70. EDWARD POYNTER (British, 1836-1919)

A Greek Girl 1892 A.P.
Photogravure on india paper
65.5 x 48.0 cm (imp.)
Signed in pencil lower left: Edward Poynter
Gift of F.M. Kimbark
Acc. no. 82/81
Printsellers' Association Stamp: MWT

Sir Edward Poynter exhibited the painting *A Greek Girl* at the Royal Academy in 1889, with the title *On the Terrace.* It was one of several small canvases of the 1880s in which he isolated one or two playful young females in idyllic classical settings. The photogravure was published in London by P. and D. Colnaghi and by Stephen Gooden in Washington. It was printed in Paris by Boussod, Valadon and Company with 250 artist's proofs. This collaboration demonstrates that the production of reproductive prints had become international in scale by the last quarter of the century.

The photogravure method was in wide use by the 1880s and 1890s. In essence, the process combined photography and engraving to make more faithful reproductions. Those who applauded the new technique claimed that,

> The mechanical nature of photogravure is distinctly in its favour for reproductive purposes; there is no opportunity for the individuality of the engraver to leave an impress on the print antagonistic to that of the painter.[56]

The process perfectly copied every brush stroke, the grain of the canvas, and details such as the painter's signature.

Most engravers were very critical of photogravure, arguing that although it reproduced the surface of the canvas, only a human interpreter could translate the real character of the painting and the intent of the artist.[57] The process, nevertheless, gradually dominated the market for reproductive engravings. A photogravure impression looked very similar to an engraving and appealed to the public, which was accustomed to the mixed-mezzotint technique and which also desired closer copies of favourite paintings. Printed in limited proof editions, photogravure had all the appeal of engraving, but at the same time represented the growing trend toward the mass-produced photomechanical reproductions of the twentieth century.

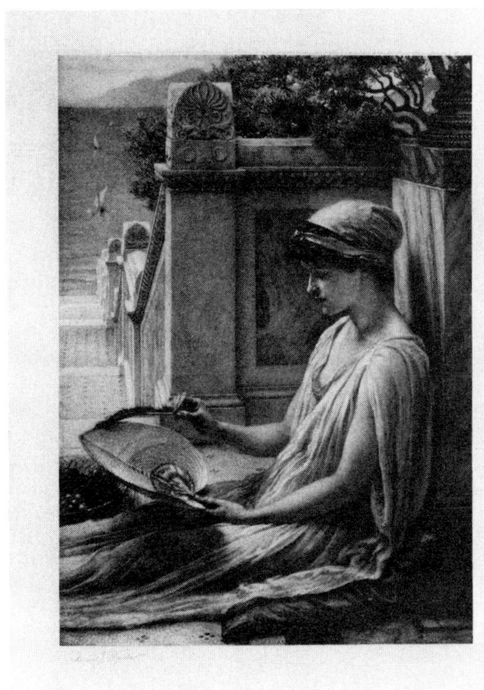

70. Poynter, *A Greek Girl*, 1892

NOTES

1. From a pamphlet written by F.G. Stephens in 1860. Quoted in Jeremy Maas, *Gambart, Prince of the Victorian Art World* (London: Barrie and Jenkins, 1975), p. 122.
2. Richard Orman, *Sir Edwin Landseer* (Philadelphia; Philadelphia Museum of Art, 1981), p.12.
3. Algernon Graves, "Engravers I have known," *The Printseller I* (January 1903): 38.
4. Richard T. Godfrey, *Printmaking in Britain* (Oxford: Phaidon Press, 1978), p. 100.
5. Seymour Haden, "About Etching," *Fine Art Quarterly* I (June 1866): 151. This article and other Haden literature were drawn to my attention by Katharine Lochnan.
6. Gerald Reitlinger, *The Economics of Taste: The Rise and Fall of Picture Prices 1760-1960* (London: Barrie and Rockcliff, 1961), p. 99.
7. N. Waddleton, "Colour Printed Supplements of the *Illustrated London News*. 1855-1896," *The Private Library* 3rd series, I (Summer 1978), 70-79.
8. For the Arundel Society, see Robyn Cooper, "The Popularization of Renaissance Art in Victorian England. The Arundel Society," *Art History* I (September 1978): 263-292. For colour printing, see R.M. Burch, *Colour Printing and Colour Printers* (London: Sir Isaac Pitman Ltd., 1910); Joan Friedman, *Colour Printing in England, 1486-1870* (New Haven: Yale Center for British Art, 1978); Ruari McClean, *Victorian Book Design and Colour Printing* (London: Faber and Faber, 1963).
9. Arthur Hayden, *Chats on Old Prints* (London: T. Fisher Unwin, 1906), p. 94.
10. "Gilbert," *Etchings, Engravings and Colour Prints* (Frost and Reed Catalogue, 1925), p. 6.
11. Richard T. Godfrey, *Printmaking in Britain*, p. 100; F.D. Klingender, *Art and the Industrial Revolution* (London: Evelyn, Adams and MacKay, 1968), pp. 174-176. Both sources illustrate and discuss the Sharples engraving in some detail.
12. See Geoffrey Wakeman, *Victorian Book Illustration: The Technical Revolution* (Great Britain: Gale Research Co., 1973), p. 30 for an illustration of a ruling machine. See Andrew W. Tuer, *Bartolozzi and his Works* (London: Field and Tuer, The Leadenhall Press, 1885), pp. 180-181 for a reference to machine rouletting.
13. Maas, *Gambart*, pp. 30-31.
14. Paul Oppé, "Art," *Early Victorian England: 1830-1865*, ed. G.M. Young (London: Oxford University Press, 1934), p. 152.
15. Noted in Maas, *Gambart*, p. 20.
16. Alfred Whitman, *Nineteenth Century Mezzotinters: Samuel Cousins, R.A.* (London: George Bell, 1904). The lives of the nineteenth-century engravers, Charles Turner and S.W. Reynolds, have also been chronicled by Whitman in separate volumes.

17. Maas, *Gambart,* p. 68.

18. Ronald Paulson, *Hogarth's Graphic Works,* vol. I (New Haven and London: Yale University Press, 1965), p. 5.

19. Noted in Maas, *Gambart,* p. 28.

20. William Plomer, "Agnew's as Publishers of Prints and Printsellers," *Agnews. 1817-1967* (London: Bradbury Agnew Press Ltd., 1967), pp. 27, 65.

21. John Burnet, "Autobiography of John Burnet," *The Art Journal* XII (1850): 276.

22. Maas, *Gambart,* p. 28.

23. *An Alphabetical List of Engravings Declared at the Office of the Printsellers' Association, London,* vol. 1, (1847-1891), p. 16.

24. *The Art Union Annual Report.* Third Annual Meeting, June 4, 1839, p. 35.

25. William Makepeace Thackery, "Letters on the Fine Arts," *Critical Papers in Art* (London: Macmillan and Co., Ltd., 1904), pp. 187-192, from *Pictorial Times,* 1843.

26. William Makepeace Thackery, "May Gambols," *Critical Papers in Art,* p. 211.

27. Elisabeth Aslin, "The Rise and Progress of the Art Union of London," *Apollo* LXXXV (January 1967): 12, 16.

28. *The Art Union Annual Report.* The 24th Annual Meeting, 1860. Quoted in Hilary Guise, *Great Victorian Engravings: A Collector's Guide* (London: Astragal Books, 1980), p. 15.

29. Philip G. Hammerton, *Etching and Etchers* (London: Macmillan and Co., Ltd., 1876), p. 365.

30. Whitman, *Samuel Cousins R.A.,* p. 24-25.

31. Sir Hubert Herkomer, *Etching and Mezzotint Engraving* (London: Macmillan and Co. Ltd., 1892), p. 93.

32. Review in the *New York Tribune,* February 6, 1883, "Dr. Haden on Etching: A Lecture at Chickering Hall."

33. See Hilary Beck, *Victorian Engravings* (London: Victoria and Albert Museum, 1973), pp. 9-11.

34. Arthur Hind, ed., *Great Engravers: John Raphael Smith and the Great Mezzotinters of the Time of Reynolds* (London: William Heinemann, 1911), p. 10.

35. C.T. Courtney Lewis, *The Picture Printer of the Nineteenth Century: George Baxter* (London: Sampson Low, Marston and Co. Ltd., 1911), p. 104.

36. Gleeson White, *English Illustration. 'The Sixties': 1855-70* (London: Archibalt Constable and Co. Ltd., 1903), p. 44.

37. For more information see Mary Lutyens, introd., *The Parables of Our Lord and Saviour Jesus Christ* (New York: Dover Publications, 1975).

38. Richard Orman, *Sir Edwin Landseer,* p. 104.

39. John Ruskin, *Modern Painters,* vol. 1, (New York: John B. Alden, Publisher, 1885), p. 75.

40. Noted in Rosemary Treble, *Great Victorian Pictures: Their Paths to Fame* (London: Arts Council of Great Britain, 1978), p. 34.

41. See Susan P. Casteras, *The Substance or the Shadow: Images of Victorian Womanhood* (New Haven: Yale Center for British Art, 1982), pp. 27-29.

42. See Casteras, p. 88 for various contemporary interpretations of the series.

43. Thomas Agnew and Sons, *Catalogue of Engravings and Etchings,* (London, 1905), p. 61.

44. Noted in Rodney Engen, *Victorian Engravings* (London: Academy Editions, 1975), p. 23.

45. The painting is now also in Royal Holloway College, University of London. The Art Gallery of Ontario has a mixed mezzotint after the painting by T.L. Atkinson.

46. Roy Strong, *And when did you last see your father? The Victorian Painter and British History* (London: Thames and Hudson, 1978), pp. 119-121.

47. The painting is currently in a private collection in New York State.

48. Sir Hubert Herkomer, *Etching,* p. 94.

49. The five paintings are now in a private collection in Italy.

50. William Powell Frith, *My Autobiography and Reminiscences* (London: Richard Bentley and Son, 1890), p. 349.

51. Hilary Guise, *Great Victorian Engravings,* p. 166 states that the fifth painting was not reproduced.

52. Frith, *My Autobiography,* p. 343.

53. Michael J. Wentworth, *James Tissot: Catalogue Raisonné of his Prints* (Minneapolis: Minneapolis Institute of Arts, 1978), p. 300.

54. The painting is in the collection of Mr. and Mrs. Joseph Tanenbaum, Toronto.

55. Wentworth, *James Tissot,* p. 25. Only 50 impressions of each etching were listed in the Tissot Vente in 1903.

56. Herbert Denison, *A Treatise on Photogravure* (London: Iliffe and Son, 1895), p. 11.

57. Herkomer, *Etching,* p. 95.

The reproductive print: copy or original?

To interpret other men's work – to render a coloured work in black and white – is a difficult art. To find the black and white that, as it were, underlies the colour; needs a fine sensitive eye.... The interpretation of pictures is an art in itself and should be judged and valued accordingly.

SIR HUBERT HERKOMER, 1892[1]

THE MAIN FUNCTION OF THE REPRODUCTIVE ENGRAVER WAS TO COPY THE original creations of other men. For this reason, debate about reproductive prints has historically focussed on the pros and cons of their value as "Art." John Ruskin (1819-1900), that great Victorian arbiter of taste, felt that they were of limited artistic importance and were of value only if they performed well as the "nurse" or "slave" to the superior schools of painting and sculpture.[2] Generally, painters and art critics conspired to assign prints to this role of handmaid and, in response, engravers self-righteously argued that engraving was as valid a form of art as painting.

At its founding in 1768 the Royal Academy found itself at the centre of this controversy when it refused to admit engravers as full Academicians. Sir Robert Strange (1721-1792), the prominent line-engraver, retaliated against this abuse by publishing *An Enquiry into the Rise and Establishment of the Royal Academy of Arts* in 1775, in which he called the Academy's position "an attack upon the art of engraving: a profession which will transmit to posterity the works of painters, when devouring time has left no traces of their pencils."[3]

Other engravers agreed with Strange and some reacted even more vehemently. John Landseer (c.1769-1852), for example, published a series of lectures in 1807 criticizing the academy for stamping engraving with "invidious and degrading inferiority."[4] In defense of reproductive prints and to emphasize the insight and innovation required by the engraver, he adopted the analogy of language, stressing that

> Engraving is no more an art of copying Painting, than the English language is an art of copying Greek or Latin. Engraving is a distinct language of Art: and

though it may bear such resemblance to Painting in the construction of its grammar, as grammars of languages bear to each other, yet its alphabet and idiom, or mode of expression, are totally different.[5]

The other analogy most often adopted to describe the differences between painting and engraving was that of music, the painter sometimes being likened to the composer of the musical score while the engraver was the performer.[6] Sir Hubert Herkomer stressed in 1892 that if done correctly an engraving should

always remind one of the entire effect of the original picture, and one should hardly miss colour. I may say with equal truth that a pianoforte arrangement of an orchestral score can be so deftly done that the effect of the instrumentation will be brought to one's mind as one hears it. This translation bears a somewhat similar relation to an orchestral score that an engraving does to a picture.[7]

Such descriptions suggest that regardless of the engraver's dedication toward making an accurate copy of the painting, reproductive prints by the very nature of the transference procedure, and the language of engraving, were always interpretive. Both Constable and Turner for example were aware of this, chosing their engravers with care, and supervising them closely. Fortunately, they found engravers with the right technique, skill, and insight to reproduce their works sympathetically. Other kindred-spirit partnerships existed in the eighteenth century between William Ryland and Angelica Kauffmann, and George Townley Stubbs and his father; in the nineteenth century, perhaps the best example was that of Samuel Cousins and John Everett Millais. These individuals recognized that reproductive prints were never replicas of the originals but were new works of art that, ideally for the painter, captured some of the intent and impact of his work in oils.

Even prints that were to a large extent facsimiles, such as eighteenth-century crayon-manner engravings or nineteenth-century wood engravings were, nevertheless, separate and unique from their models. In an article on the engravings of Marcantonio Raimondi, Colin Eisler stressed the paradox that exists for all reproductive prints: they are both copies of originals and originals or new art objects at the same time.[8] They give the viewer information about works of art, which one often assumes is accurate and reveals all necessary facts about the original; in this way they can be cleverly deceptive. It is quite possible for reproductive prints to distort or change the intention of the painter. Whether the engraver subtracts or adds details (in most examples, the latter is true because of the nature of the techniques); or whether he idealizes or depreciates the subject, changes are inevitably made, however subtle. The engraver works essentially with a black-and-white linear vocabulary, hence there is a tendency for a gaily coloured painting to become somber in translation, and for a softly modelled image to become sharply defined. He has to approximate shadow and texture through a proliferation of lines and dots with no exact equivalent for brush-work or impasto. The result of the transition is that the viewer must deal with an object that recalls or reminds him of the model but that also conveys new information not found in the original painting.

John Barrell's examination of the work of the eighteenth-century painter George Morland illustrates this fact. Mr. Barrell concludes that Morland's engravers consistently misrepresented the painter's intention by idealizing and emasculating his images, making them prettier and more picturesque.[9] The engravings subsequently influenced people's judgement of the artistic worth of Morland's painting.

It is quite possible that other prints have also affected historical and modern assessment of the purposes and accomplishments of certain painters. Ruskin, with his albeit biased view of engraving, lamented that people were "misled into attributing to the painter himself qualities impertinently added by the engraver to make his plate popular: and... [were] gradually and subtly prevented from looking, in the original, for the qualities which engraving could never render."[10] Certainly, it is well documented that very diverse conclusions have been drawn about sight-unseen Old Master paintings, drawings and sculptures, based on the available prints.[11]

At the same time that engravers were popularizing their images, artists may have been conditioning their styles of painting by the requirements of the print. Many paintings were designed specifically to be engraved, for example, the fancy subjects of Cipriani and Kauffmann and the Boydell Shakespeare series. Other painters, however, including such eminent figures as Sir Joshua Reynolds in the eighteenth century and the Pre-Raphaelite circle in the nineteenth, have been accused of allowing the dictates of contemporary engraving to influence their approaches to the canvas.[12] Further exploration in this area might enhance our knowledge of the development of British painting during the period.

The exhibition has tried to emphasize the popular aspect of reproductive prints in their role as barometers of taste. However, to examine the way in which they may have influenced painting styles and to understand their capacity as information-bearers to wide audiences – conditioning the way artists, art historians, and the general public have thought about art – requires a great deal more comparison of large numbers of related paintings and prints. Recognition of largely uncharted areas of study suggest that the value of reproductive prints to the history of art extends beyond their qualification as art. Perhaps in the future the reproductive print will be discussed in a broader context, one in which the position of its maker as popularizer and interpreter, as well as artist, may take on new meaning and importance.

NOTES

1. Sir Hubert Herkomer, *Etching and Mezzotint Engraving* (London: Macmillan and Co., Ltd., 1892), pp. 92, 102.
2. John Ruskin, *Ariadne Fiorentina: Six Lectures on Wood and Metal Engraving* (New York: John B. Alden, 1885), p.24.
3. Sir Robert Strange, *An Enquiry into the Rise and Establishment of the Royal Academy of Arts* (London: E. and C. Dilly, 1775), p. 112.
4. John Landseer, *Lectures on the Art of Engraving* (London: Longman, Hurst, Rees and Orme, 1807), p. 325.
5. Ibid., p. 177.
6. Andrew W. Tuer, *Bartolozzi and his Works* (London: Field and Tuer, The Leadenhall Press, 1885), p. 164.
7. Herkomer, *Etching*, p. 96.
8. Colin Eisler, "Marcantonio: The Reproductive Print as Paradox," *The Print Collector's Newsletter*, XIII, (July-August 1982): 80.
9. John Barrell, *The Dark Side of the Landscape: The Rural Poor in English Painting 1730-1840* (Cambridge: Cambridge University Press, 1980), pp. 93, 120-122.
10. Ruskin, *Ariadne Fiorentina*, p. 141-142.
11. William M. Ivins, *Prints and Visual Communication* (Cambridge, Mass.: MIT Press, 1980, first pub. 1953), p. 89. In this example, Ivins describes the disparity among engravings of the Laocoon.
12. Richard T. Godfrey, *Printmaking in Britain* (Oxford: Phaidon Press, 1978), p. 48. Paul Oppé, "Art," *Early Victorian England: 1830-1865*, ed. G.M. Young (London: Oxford University Press, 1934), p. 148.

TRANSFERRING THE IMAGE FROM THE CANVAS TO THE METAL PLATE

The transference of the image from the canvas to the metal plate was undoubtedly a challenge for all engravers. The evidence as to how this was accomplished is somewhat sketchy, particularly for the earlier period.

Whenever possible, the original painting was kept in the engraver's studio for constant reference while he was working on the plate. If the painting was very large, a reduced version in oil made by the painter, the engraver, or an assistant was used as a model (see nos. 12 and 13). In addition, the painter was often available for consultation; this is illustrated by Boydell's announcement in a 1769 advertisement for engravings that the painters were "both able and willing to give the Engraver all the necessary Advice and Assistance he can require."[1]

At the outset a decision was made, either by the painter or the engraver, about the reversal of the image. Occasionally, the composition was transferred directly to the plate without being drawn in reverse; the resulting engraving was therefore the mirror image of the original painting (see No. 26 and fig. 3). Most often, in order to provide a correct reading of the narrative elements or to retain the compositional balance, the image was reversed on the plate so that the engraving would be printed in the same direction as the painting (see No. 12 and fig. 2). A number of specialized technical procedures as well as a large mirror were important aids for the engraver in this reversal.

According to several writers, a very precise and detailed drawing the size of the copper plate was prepared by "squaring up" the canvas, often using cotton threads which were stretched at right angles to each other across the painting, creating a horizontal and vertical grid.[2] The paper was then squared up and the painting copied square by square. Algernon Graves remembered visiting an engraver's studio in the mid-nineteenth century and finding the original painting "covered with a network of cotton squares... to facilitate accurate copying."[3] Black or white watercolour, depending on the ground colour of the painting, was also used to perform this function. The engraver could draw a grid on the canvas with watercolour, which could be easily washed off.[4] The small size of the squares and the numbering of each square assured the most accurate copy possible.[5]

Methods for transferring the image from the drawing to the plate varied among engravers. The engraver could cover the back of the drawing with red chalk and place this side down on the plate. When the lines of the drawing were re-traced, they were transferred in red to the plate.[6] This method, however, would not result in reversal. Alternatively, the drawing could be executed on tracing paper and the engraver, by looking through the back of the paper, could reverse the image on the plate.[7] These two methods were probably used most often for eighteenth-century mezzotints, since preliminary etching in most other print media allowed for an easier procedure. When an etching ground was used, the drawing could be dampened and placed face-down on the waxed surface of the plate and passed through the press as in printing. The pencil marks were transferred to the waxed surface and the image was reversed.[8] The plate could then be etched and details added, using the selected method, by referring to both the drawing and the painting. In the nineteenth century, photographs of the original often provided further models.[9]

The published engraving was the result of the efforts of several skilled men, including the "copyist," possibly the engraver himself, who made the detailed drawing of the original; the engraver and his assistants, who engraved the plate and prepared it for printing; the specialist writing engraver, who added the lettering; and the professional printer, who ran the press and expertly pulled each impression. In the eighteenth century the length of time required to complete one line-engraving on copper was at least three years, although mezzotint and stipple demanded less time.[10] With the sophisticated mechanical aids and the number of assistants employed in nineteenth-century engraving studios, the prints often appeared only a year or less after the initial exhibition of the painting (see nos. 55, 61, 62).

NOTES

1. John Boydell, *Boydell's Sculptura Britannica: A Collection of Prints, Engraved after the most Capital Paintings in England. Volume First.* 1769, p. 3-4. Quoted in David Alexander, "Painters and Engràving from Reynolds to Wilkie," *The Connoisseur* CC (January 1979): 61.

2. Theodore Henry Fielding, *The Art of Engraving, with the Various Modes of Operation* (London: Ackermann and Co., 1841), p. 18.

   W.G. Rawlinson, "Notes Chiefly on the Technique of Mezzotint Engraving," *The Burlington Fine Arts Club Exhibition of English Mezzotint Portraits from circa 1750-circa 1830* (London: Chiswick Press: Charles Wittingham and Co., 1902), p. 15.

   Arthur Hayden, *Chats on Old Prints* (London: Fisher Unwin, 1906), p. 209.

   P.H. Martindale, *Engraving, Old and Modern* (London: Heath Cranton Ltd., 1928), p. 153-154.

3. Algernon Graves, "Engravers I have known" *The Printseller,* I (January 1903): 37.

4. Fielding, *The Art of Engraving*, p. 18.

5. Martindale, *Engraving*, p. 153.

6. Martindale, *Engraving*, p. 153: David Alexander and Richard T. Godfrey, *Painters and Engraving: The Reproductive Print from Hogarth to Wilkie* (New Haven: Yale Center for British Art, 1980), p. 8.

7. Antony Griffiths, "Prints after Reynolds and Gainsborough," *Gainsborough and Reynolds in the British Museum* (London: British Museum Publications, 1978), p. 30.

8. Fielding, *The Art of Engraving*, p. 18.

9. Graves, "Engravers I have known," p. 37. Jeremy Maas, *Gambart, Prince of the Victorian Art World* (London: Barrie and Jenkins, 1975), p. 158. Maas quotes William P. Frith who promises that he will "touch up" photographs to assist the engravers of his paintings.

10. William Sharp, letter to Charles Warren, dated 29th May, 1810. Published in H.C. Levis, *A Descriptive Bibliography of the Most Important Books in the English Language Relating to the Art and History of Engraving* (London: Ellis, 1912), p. 96.

PRINTMAKING TECHNIQUES

Traditional printmaking techniques fall into three basic categories: the **intaglio** processes, in which the design is sunk below the surface; the **relief** processes, in which the design is raised above the surface; and the **planographic** process of lithography, in which the design remains in the same plane as the surface. The majority of reproductive prints made in England between 1775 and 1900 fall into the intaglio category, although lithography and the relief technique, wood-engraving, were used extensively to make special kinds of reproductions.

INTAGLIO PROCESSES

For all intaglio processes, the traditional printing surface is copper although the harder metal, steel, which guaranteed extremely large editions, was introduced in the 1820s and used throughout the nineteenth century (p. 57). By the 1860s copper was reinstated for many prints because **steel-facing**, a process in which a thin coating of steel was deposited on the surface of the copper plate by electrolysis, made virtually unlimited editions possible (p. 63).

To prepare the copper or steel plate for printing, lines are incised with a burin (line-engraving) or bitten with acid (etching) into the metal surface. Ink is then rubbed into the lines and the plate wiped clean. Dampened paper is placed on the plate, which is run under a heavy roller. The pressure forces the paper into the lines where it picks up the ink.

Line-Engraving

The term **engraving** can be applied in a general sense to most intaglio techniques, although it more specifically applies to line-engraving. In line-engraving, the design is incised on a metal plate with a square or lozenge-shaped gouge called a **burin** or a **graver.** The process requires great manual control and years of training to master an elaborate system of lines, dots, and cross-hatchings. Line-engraving was widely held to be superior to other printmaking techniques and was used in the late eighteenth century to reproduce grand, historical subjects (No. 10). With the demand for quick production and the advent of steel plates in the nineteenth century, line-engraving gradually declined. The hardness of the new metal resulted in fine, shallow lines that were appropriate for small illustrations but not for large plates. Eventually, traditional line-engraving became almost obsolete.

Drypoint

In drypoint, the image is scratched lightly on the plate using a sharp stylus made of steel or diamond. The **drypoint needle** does not remove copper from the plate but displaces a curl of copper **burr** on either side of the lines. In printing, the lines have a velvety appearance. The burr wears quickly in printing, making it difficult to pull large editions. Drypoint is primarily a painter's medium used to make original prints. It is sometimes found in reproductive prints, where it strengthens engraved or etched lines (No. 68). On mezzotint plates, it was occasionally used for details or to scratch in the lettering on proof impressions (No. 2).

Mezzotint

Mezzotint is a tonal rather than a linear process and was used extensively to reproduce oil paintings. To prepare the plate, a tool called a **rocker,** which has a semi-circular steel blade with a serrated edge, is rocked carefully in at least twenty directions over the surface. The teeth make myriads of tiny tapered holes in the plate, at the same time that a small fleck of burr is raised on the edge of each hole. If the plate were inked and printed at this point, it would yield a uniform black tone over the entire surface of the impression. The engraver must work from dark to light to create the image by scraping and burnishing away the copper wherever he wants highlights.

The technique was used almost exclusively in England and came to be called ***la manière anglaise*** (p. 16). It is found in its pure form in eighteenth century portrait mezzotints (nos. 1-2). In the nineteenth century it was often combined on the plate with linear techniques, especially etching (nos. 4, 34-35). Later in the century, the mixed-mezzotint process, in which the foundation was mezzotint and other techniques were added to the plate, was used to reproduce popular paintings (nos. 50-54, 58-62; see *Mixed Method*).

Etching

In etching, the plate is coated with a thin, waxy **ground** which is impervious to strong acid. The etcher then draws through the ground with an **etching needle** and exposes the copper beneath. The plate is immersed in acid and "bitten" or etched. After the etching process is completed, the plate is taken out of the acid and the ground is removed with solvent.

Unlike line-engraving, etching does not require years of technical training and partly for this reason, along with its characteristic freedom of line, it was used in its pure form primarily for original designs. In reproductive prints it often provided the foundation on the plate for line-engraving, mezzotint, or stipple (nos. 14-15, 41-42). With the revival of pure etching at the end of the nineteenth century, many etchers entered the lucrative field of reproductive prints, using the technique in a careful and systematic way to copy oil paintings rather than in the more usual spontaneous manner (nos. 63-68).

Soft-Ground Etching

In soft-ground etching, tallow is mixed with the etching wax and this **soft ground** is applied to the plate. A sheet of paper is laid on this surface and a drawing in chalk or graphite is made on the paper. When the paper is lifted off, the ground adheres to it wherever the lines were drawn and the copper is exposed beneath. The plate is bitten in acid as in ordinary etching, but the resulting impressions are very similar in appearance to chalk or graphite sketches. The technique was used in the late eighteenth century to reproduce original drawings (No. 31).

Crayon-Manner and Stipple

In the crayon-manner, a plate covered with an etching ground is punctured with dots of various sizes, made primarily by **roulettes,** instruments with tooth-wheels of various kinds that are rolled over the plate to create dotted lines. Other tools that similarly perforate the surface were also employed. The plate is bitten as in etching and a burin is often used for additional dotting before printing. The process was invented in France to imitate chalk and crayon drawings and was brought to England by William Ryland in the 1760s (No. 5).

Stipple employed the same tools as the crayon-manner but expanded their use to reproduce oil paintings and watercolours, as well as drawings. The soft tonal values were particularly suited to quiet, pastoral subjects and the stipple technique became very popular for decorative wall-prints (nos. 18, 21-24). Its greatest exponent at the end of the eighteenth century was Bartolozzi (p. 19). In the early nineteenth century both the crayon-manner and stipple were superseded by lithography. In the Victorian period stipple was used in combination with etching, line-engraving, and mezzotint for mixed-method engraving.

Aquatint

Like the mezzotint and stipple processes, aquatint is essentially tonal rather than linear. To prepare the plate, powdered **resin** or asphaltum powder is fused to the plate by heat. This leaves minute interstices that, when bitten by acid, result in a finely pitted surface. Areas of white can be preserved by brushing on a varnish. The technique was invented in France and used in England in the late eighteenth century by Paul Sandby to approximate the effects of wash drawings (No. 30).

Sandby and Gainsborough also employed a special process called **sugar-lift** or **lift-ground aquatint.** This involves brushing the design on the plate with a mixture of Indian ink and sugar and then covering the plate with varnish. Upon immersion in water, the sugar expands and lifts the varnish off the plate, exposing the copper. The plate is then etched in the normal manner.

Mixed Method

George Stubbs' prints after his own paintings are described as "engravings by mixed methods" because he used several intaglio techniques on each plate (nos. 27-28). A distinction should be made between his creative and careful manipulation of techniques and the highly finished, glossy surfaces of nineteenth-century mixed-method engravings. The latter were the result of a growing effort to reproduce accurately the qualities of contemporary oil painting. Any number of intaglio techniques were used on the plate, most often built up on a tonal mezzotint foundation (nos. 50-62). Mixed-method engravings were the most prestigious prints of the Victorian period. Editions appeared in an array of impressions, from signed **artist's proofs** (in the catalogue entries, **A.P.**) to unlettered and lettered prints, the rarest of which were printed on a fine paper called **india paper.**

Colour Printing

The most common method of colour printing in the late eighteenth century was called ***à la poupée*** and was used extensively for stipples (nos. 7, 20, 21-22). The plate was inked by carefully "dabbing on" several colours in appropriate locations and by a single run through the press the image was printed in colour. Often the final prints were touched up using hand-colouring. In the nineteenth century, a number of other colour printing methods were introduced, including George Baxter's oil-colour prints (no. 45) and chromolithography (p. 56).

OTHER REPRODUCTIVE PROCESSES

Lithography

Invented in 1798, the process is based on the natural antithesis of oil and water. It involves drawing on certain kinds of smooth, porous stone with a special type of wax pencil. The stone, prepared using acid, gum arabic, and water, accepts ink applied with a roller to the drawn areas, but repels the ink over the rest of its dampened surface. In England, lithography supplanted stipple and aquatint in the early nineteenth century, especially in the area of topographical watercolours and drawings. It was much criticized by John Ruskin, and was felt to be tainted with commercialism. Most painters preferred the more prestigious intaglio techniques for the reproduction of their works in oil.

Wood Engraving

In wood engraving the end-grain of a hard wood is used for the printing surface. A burin, almost identical to the line-engraver's burin, incises fine lines into the wood block. Although the technique is called wood engraving it falls into the relief category because the raised surface is inked; the incised lines, therefore, print white and not black as in the intaglio process. The expanding market for books and periodicals in the nineteenth century fostered several important wood engraving firms (nos. 46-47).

Photomechanical Processes

Photography was one of the great inventions of the nineteenth century and had a direct or indirect effect on all printmaking during the second half of the century, particularly in the field of book illustration. It was used in various combinations with traditional engraving techniques, metal relief plates, wood engraving, and lithography. By the 1890s photomechanical processes completely eliminated the need for the reproductive engraver.

Photogravure was a photomechanical process that had much of the appeal of mixed-method engraving along with an extraordinary tonal range (No. 70). The process consists of transferring the photographed image, in the form of a negative contacted to carbon tissue, to a metal plate that has been treated with an aquatint ground. The plate is etched in an acid bath, after which further touch up work by a skilled artisan is possible. The plate is printed on the usual engraving press. Photogravure was distinct among photomechanical processes because it left a **plate-mark** (the impression - **imp.** - of the plate on the paper caused by the pressure of the printing press) and because it was most responsible for the demise of mixed-method engraving in the late nineteenth century.

PRINCIPAL CATALOGUES RAISONNÉS WITH ABBREVIATIONS

B. BAKER, W.S. *William Sharp, Engraver.* Philadelphia: Gebbie and Barrie Pub., 1875.

BM STEPHENS, F.G., and GEORGE, M.D. *Catalogue of Political and Personal Satires, Preserved in the Department of Prints and Drawings in the British Museum.* 11 vols. London: British Museum, 1870-1954.

C. and V. CALABI, A., and DE VESME, A. *Francesco Bartolozzi.* Milan: Guido Modiano, 1928.

C.S. CHALONER SMITH, John. *British Mezzotinto Portraits.* 4 vols. London: Henry Sotheran and Co., 1878-1883.

F FAGAN, L. *A Catalogue Raisonné of the Engraved Works of William Woollett.* London: The Fine Art Society, 1885.

Le B. LE BLANC, Charles. *Catalogue de l'oeuvre de Robert Strange.* Leipzig, 1848.

P. PRESSLY, William. *The Life and Art of James Barry.* New Haven and London: Yale University Press, 1981.

R. RAWLINSON, W.G. *The Engraved Work of J.M.W. Turner.* 2 vols. London: Macmillan and Co., 1908-1913.

R. RAWLINSON, W.G. *Turner's Liber Studiorum: A Description and a Catalogue.* London: Macmillan and Co., 1878.

S. SHIRLEY, Andrew. *The Published Mezzotints of David Lucas after John Constable R.A.* London: Oxford at the Clarendon Press, 1930.

T. TAYLOR, Basil. *The Prints of George Stubbs.* London: Phaidon Press, 1971.

W. WEBSTER, Mary. *Francis Wheatley.* London: The Paul Mellon Foundation for British Art, 1970.

W. WENTWORTH, Michael J. *James Tissot: Catalogue Raisonné of his Prints.* Minneapolis: Minneapolis Institute of Arts, 1978.

W. WHITMAN, Alfred. *Nineteenth Century Mezzotinters: Samuel Cousins, R.A.* London: George Bell, 1904.

W. WHITMAN, Alfred. *Nineteenth Century Mezzotinters: Charles Turner.* London: George Bell, 1907.

SELECTED BIBLIOGRAPHY

ALEXANDER, David, and GODFREY, Richard T. *Painters and Engraving: The Reproductive Print from Hogarth to Wilkie.* New Haven: Yale Center for British Art, 1980. Exhibition Catalogue.

ALEXANDER, David. "Painters and Engraving from Reynolds to Wilkie." *The Connoisseur CC* (January 1979): 58-64.

An Alphabetical List of Engravings Declared at the Office of the Printsellers' Association, London, vol. 1, 1847-1891; vol. 2, 1892-1911.

ASHWIN, Clive. "Graphic Imagery 1837-1901: A Victorian Revolution." *Art History* I (September 1978): 360-370.

BECK, Hilary. *Victorian Engravings.* London: Victoria and Albert Museum, 1973. Exhibition Catalogue.

BOASE, Thomas. S.R. *English Art, 1800-1870.* Oxford: Clarendon Press, 1959.

BURNET, John. *Practical Essays on Various Branches of the Fine Arts.* London: David Bogue, 1848.

CATE, Phillip Dennis, and SPECTOR, Jack. *Circa 1800. The Beginnings of Modern Printmaking 1775-1835.* New Brunswick, New Jersey: Rutgers University Art Gallery, 1981. Exhibition Catalogue.

ENGEN, Rodney K. *Dictionary of Victorian Engravers, Print Publishers and Their Works.* Cambridge: Chadwyck-Healey, 1979.

ENGEN, Rodney K. *Victorian Engravings.* London: Academy Editions, 1975.

FIELDING, Theodore Henry. *The Art of Engraving, with the Various Modes of Operation.* London: Ackermann and Co., 1841.

FRANKAU, Julia. *Eighteenth Century Colour Prints: an Essay on Certain Stipple Engravers and their work in Colour.* London: Macmillan and Co. Ltd., 1906, first published in 1900.

FRIEDMAN, Winifred *Boydell's Shakespeare Gallery.* New York and London: Garland Publishing Inc., 1976.

GARLICK, Kenneth, and MACINTYRE, Angus, eds. *The Diary of Joseph Farington.* 8 vols., (from June, 1793 - December, 1804) and Kathryn Cave, ed. (from January, 1805 - December, 1807). New Haven and London: Yale University Press, 1978-82.

GODFREY, Richard T. *Printmaking in Britain.* Oxford: Phaidon Press, 1978.

GRAY, Basil. *The English Print.* London: Adam and Charles Black, 1937.

GRAVES, Algernon. *The Royal Academy of Arts: A Complete Dictionary of Contributors and Their Work from its Foundation in 1769 to 1904.* 4 vols. London: Henry Graves & George Bell, 1905-6.

GRIFFITHS, Antony. "Prints after Reynolds and Gainsborough." *Gainsborough and Reynolds in the British Museum.* London: British Museum Publications, 1978.

GRIFFITHS, Antony. *Prints and Printmaking.* London: British Museum Publications, 1980.

GUISE, Hilary. *Great Victorian Engravings: A Collector's Guide.* London: Astragal Books, 1980.

HERKOMER, Sir Hubert. *Etching and Mezzotint Engraving.* London: Macmillan and Co. Ltd., 1892.

HIND, Arthur M. *A History of Engraving and Etching.* New York: Dover Publications, 1963, first published in 1908.

IVINS, William M. *Prints and Visual Communication.* Cambridge, Mass.: MIT Press, 1980, first published in 1953.

LANDSEER, John. *Lectures on the Art of Engraving.* London: Longman, Hurst, Rees and Orme, 1807.

LLOYD, C.H. *Art and Its Images: An Exhibition of Printed Books Containing Engraved Illustrations after Italian Paintings.* Oxford: The Bodelian Library, 1975. Exhibition Catalogue.

MAAS, Jeremy. *Gambart, Prince of the Victorian Art World.* London: Barrie and Jenkins, 1975.

MAAS, Jeremy. *Victorian Painters.* London: Barrie and Rockcliff, The Cresset Press, 1969.

PRIDEAUX, S.T. *Aquatint Engraving.* London: Duckworth and Co., 1909.

PYE, John. *Patronage of British Art.* London: Longman, Brown, Green and Longmans, 1845.

REDGRAVE, Samuel, *A Dictionary of Artists of the English School.* London: first pub. 1874, facsimile reprint, Kingsmead Reprints, 1970.

REYNOLDS, Graham. *Victorian Painting.* London: Studio Vista Ltd., 1966.

RUSKIN, John. *Ariadne Fiorentina: Six Lectures on Wood and Metal Engraving.* New York: John B. Alden, 1885.

TUER, Andrew W. *Bartolozzi and his Works.* London: Field and Tuer, The Leadenhall Press, 1885.

WAKEMAN, Geoffrey. *Victorian Book Illustration: The Technical Revolution.* Great Britain: Gale Research Co., 1973.

WATERHOUSE, Ellis. *Painting in Britain, 1530-1790.* London and Baltimore: Penguin Books Ltd., 2nd ed., 1962.

WHITLEY, William T. *Artists and Their Friends in England 1700-1799.* 2 vols. London and Boston: The Medici Society, 1928.

WHITMAN, Alfred. *Masters of Mezzotint: The Men and Their Work.* London: George Bell, 1898.

INDEX OF ARTISTS AND TITLES